PROSTITUTION
AND THE
VICTORIANS

An idealised vision of commercial sex. (Mary Evans Picture Library)

PROSTITUTION
AND THE
VICTORIANS

Trevor Fisher

SUTTON PUBLISHING

ST. MARTIN'S PRESS, NEW YORK

First published in the United Kingdom in 1997 by
Sutton Publishing Limited · Phoenix Mill
Thrupp · Stroud · Gloucestershire · GL5 2BU

First published in the United States by St. Martin's Press
Scholarly and Reference Division
175 Fifth Avenue · New York · N.Y. 10010

British Library Cataloguing in Publication Data
A catalogue record for this book is available from the British Library

ISBN 0 7509 1125 5

Library of Congress Cataloging-in-Publication Data applied for

ISBN 0 312 17583 3

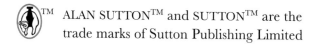 ALAN SUTTON™ and SUTTON™ are the
trade marks of Sutton Publishing Limited

Typeset in 11/14pt Baskerville.
Typesetting and origination by
Sutton Publishing Limited.
Printed in Great Britain by
Hartnolls, Bodmin, Cornwall.

Contents

To Sarah, with love

Introduction: Raising the Veil

Historical views of Victorian morality have long been shaped by a double image. For many, the Victorian period sees the triumph of middle class respectability. From this perspective, Queen Victoria was the middle class monarch of a middle class society. The bourgeois values of a Protestant work ethic went hand in hand with moral virtue, the sanctity of marriage, and sex as a means of procreation. Countering this image of respectability, critics from Bernard Shaw and Lytton Strachey onward have painted a more negative picture. They stigmatised Victorian values as prudish, repressive and hypocritical. This tradition has emphasised the existence of the sexual double standard, sexual exploitation and the widespread use of female prostitutes.

The double image represents two sides of the same coin, and it is a moot point among historians which image represents the more dominant reality. There is little doubt that there was a real shift in attitudes and behaviour during the nineteenth century. Attitudes changed from the rakishness of the Regency period, when the scandalous behaviour of George IV and his brother William IV seemed to set the tone for whole sections of the upper classes, to a dominant bourgeois respectability half a century later. Victoria and her beloved Prince Albert appeared to be perfect exemplars of the morality of a rising middle class which after 1832 enjoyed the fruits of political power.

But however real the shifts in attitude, there is little doubt that there was widespread sexual license among respectable males even when Victoria and Albert were exhibiting the virtues of wedded bliss. This is demonstrated beyond contention by the existence of prostitution on a scale which was compared unfavourably with Continental Europe. 'I am afraid', Gladstone told the House of Commons in 1857, 'as respects the gross evils of prostitution, that there is hardly any country in the world where they prevail to a greater extent than in our own.'[1] Howard Vincent, the Director of the Criminal Investigation Department at Scotland Yard, made a similar point to the House of Lords select committee investigating white slavery in 1881, stating that 'I should think that prostitution in England is considerably in excess of the prostitution in other countries.'[2] Both men spoke from experience. Gladstone walked the streets of London seeking to reclaim prostitutes, while Vincent worked at the head of a police network extending deep into the seamiest areas of London.

Although female prostitution was massively visible on the streets of nineteenth-century Britain, both contemporaries and historians have found it easy to avert their eyes. For most respectable Victorians, the situation was simply unmentionable, and mainstream historians have tended to follow their lead. Neither of the two Oxford Histories of England which cover the period confront the phenomenon or its political effects. Llewellyn Woodward, in the volume which covers 1815 to 1870, has one index entry on prostitution, and this refers only to a brief footnote. Robert Ensor, writing on England from 1870 to 1914, has no index entry at all. Yet the invisibility of prostitution for mainstream historians is not determined by a lack of historical material.

The 'Great Social Evil', as contemporaries called it, may have been unmentionable in polite society but this was certainly not the case among politicians, medical experts, campaigning newspaper editors or religious activists. Prostitution was too widespread a phenomenon to be swept under the carpet, and throughout the nineteenth century a remarkable amount of evidence about female prostitution and its effects emerged. Government reports, pamphlets from moral and medical campaigners, newspaper articles, debates in the Commons and the Lords, and the ephemera from a wide range of public agitations, testify to a widespread and serious debate. With the high-minded seriousness and almost obsessive concern with detail characteristic of nineteenth-century social investigation, female prostitution and its effects were repeatedly probed and assessed.

This book focuses on this important discourse and its legislative effects, using the words of the participants to illustrate a debate which penetrated some of the darkest areas of nineteenth-century life. So much material exists that no single volume can claim to be exhaustive. What is attempted here is a selective examination of the contemporary debate on prostitution in the 'long' nineteenth century, from around 1790 to 1914, the extracts selected being set in their broad historical context.

I detect three phases in debate over this period. In the first, from the 1790s to the Act of 1849, the moral purity campaign associated with the Society for the Suppression of Vice sought both to publicise the problem of prostitution while campaigning for strict police action against brothels and street-walkers. Starting with Patrick Colquhoun in the 1790s, puritans attempted to estimate the number of prostitutes in major cities, assess the nature and effects of the market in commercial sex, and use the evidence gleaned by painstaking investigation to force the government to change the law in favour of repression. These early investigations failed to produce anything like a plausible estimate of numbers, some of their estimates being so hopelessly exaggerated as to invite ridicule. Nevertheless they demonstrated a problem of considerable size and social impact. Most early investigators were zealots, but independent foreign observers corroborated the existence of a phenomenon which seemed to them to be on an extraordinary scale for so overtly religious a country.

But no matter how much evidence was presented to the government, the

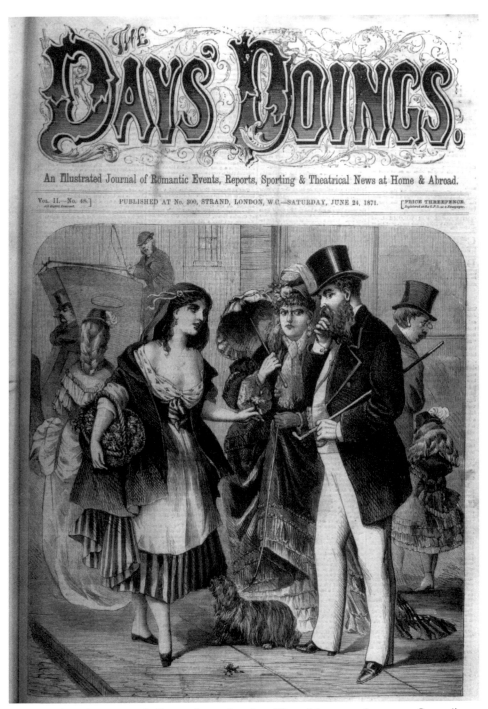

An awkward encounter in Regent Street, London: 'That girl seems to know you, George!'
(*The Day's Doings*, vol. 2, 24 June 1871, p. 353. Mary Evans Picture Library)

authorities remained unmoved. Acts were passed in 1824, 1839 and 1849 to tighten the legal code, but none infringed the right of women to sell their bodies, or their clients to buy. The only effective legislation proposed in this period, the Bishop of Exeter's Act of 1844, was destroyed by a government offensive led by the formidable Duke of Wellington. This was the high season of *laissez-faire* economics, and neither government nor magistrates were prepared to restrict the market in sexual favours. Nor did the attitude change over the next forty years. When Howard Vincent was interviewed by the House of Lords select committee in 1881, his opinion was that 'The police are absolutely powerless as regards prostitution in London.'[3] This was something of an exaggeration, but not far from the truth. Police powers were so hedged about with restrictions as to make them virtually unenforceable. Ministers regularly met with moral purity deputations and equally regularly deplored the disgraceful state of morality revealed by moral purity investigations. They were, however, unwilling to do anything about it.

By 1850 moral purity had run out of steam. A second phase of the debate developed as the initiative was steadily taken by people who believed that prostitution could not be abolished or suppressed. This utilitarian current believed that prostitution should be regulated by the state, with licensed brothels supervised by a morals police, following the practice on the Continent. The system used in France and Belgium was well known among affluent middle class males, since many of them took advantage of it themselves. The impetus toward state regulation of prostitution came principally from the public health lobby, although the first substantial discussion of regulation came from the pen of the conservative writer W.R. Greg in 1850.

The public health lobby had secured the first legislative victory against *laissez-faire* in the 1848 Act providing state action against the recurrent epidemics of cholera that ravaged Victorian Britain. Lobbyists looked on venereal disease in much the same light as cholera, considering prostitutes to be little more than carriers of disease that could be controlled in the same way as the contaminated water supplies which carried cholera. State regulation on the Continental model was the ultimate aim, but in the 1850s and 1860s lobbyists found their most productive line of advance was to play on fears in government and military circles about the impact of venereal disease on the fighting efficiency of the army and navy. Following the disasters of the Crimean War, this had become a major issue in Whitehall. The high command found venereal disease a convenient scapegoat for military failure, and their pressure on government opened the way to the regulation of prostitution in naval and garrison towns via three Contagious Diseases Acts in 1864, 1866 and 1869, which were intended to supply disease-free women for the other ranks. These three Acts convinced the public health lobby that a Continental-style system applied to the civilian population was within their grasp. Their hopes were to be dashed. A fierce puritan reaction to the Acts developed, ushering in the third and final phase of the debate on prostitution.

The passing of the 1869 Act goaded moral puritans into forming a far more effective lobby than they had produced in the 1840s. The campaign against the Contagious Diseases Acts which developed after the 1869 Act united moralists and proto-feminists. Both groups protested against women being regulated in deeply personal matters while their clients went free. Moreover, in the person of Josephine Butler, the campaign discovered a leader of outstanding ability. The initial stages of the campaign, launched against Gladstone's first ministry, displayed an intransigence which alienated potential supporters, but by the time Gladstone returned to power in 1880 the campaign against the CD Acts had learnt from these mistakes and had become a formidable pressure group.

To many Gladstonians, particularly non-conformist Liberals, the Contagious Diseases Acts and their *de facto* creation of a morals police created serious moral and political dilemmas. Nevertheless, the campaign against the CD Acts encountered massive resistance. The decisive moves toward puritanism only came when moral purity activists discovered white slavery – the forcible detention of British women in state brothels on the Continent. Even then, the puritans only succeeded in outlawing the traffic by virtue of an extraordinary press offensive fought by W.T. Stead, the crusading editor of the *Pall Mall Gazette*. In the summer of 1885 Stead published a series of sensational articles under the banner of 'The Maiden Tribute of Modern Babylon', claiming that the government was turning its back on massive sexual abuse. Stead's campaign forced the government to rush through the Criminal Law Amendment Act of 1885, a comprehensive puritanical measure which secured all that the moral purity lobby had been seeking throughout the century.

With the passage of this Act, the initiative passed decisively to moral purity. The advocates of regulation of prostitution by the state were defeated, and they remain a marginal force over a century later. The moral purity lobby formed a new and powerful campaign organisation, the National Vigilance Association, which disdained mere investigation and debating of prostitution. The NVA existed to enforce the advantage puritans had gained with the new law. A successful crusade against brothels transformed police attitudes, leading to closures en masse across the country. One reason why 'Jack the Ripper' found murdering prostitutes a simple matter in Whitechapel in 1888 was that NVA zealots had driven prostitutes to service their clients in the back alleys of slum streets, where they were easy prey for the sadistic killer.

By the last decade of Victoria's reign, Victorian values had taken on their most characteristic form regarding prostitution. Prostitution *per se* had not been criminalised, nor was it ever. But both the law and police behaviour had become so repressive that brothels could only operate under strict conditions of secrecy, and through the hazardous procedure of bribing police officers. Street-walking became a high-risk activity for both prostitutes and their clients. Two articulate and well-connected men,

Ray Lankester, Professor of Anatomy at Oxford University, and George Alexander, the theatrical producer of Pinero and Oscar Wilde, fell foul of the law in the 1890s and found themselves in the dock for alleged relations with prostitutes. They proclaimed their innocence in *The Times*, claiming that the police had behaved in an outrageously illiberal way. Their protests made little difference. The Vagrancy Act of 1898, aimed at pimps who lived off immoral earnings, completed a formidable legal weaponry for the police to use. Repression had become dominant.

But as the critics of Victorian values correctly argue, this is not the full story. This third stage of the debate on prostitution enshrined a particularly strait-laced view of prostitution, but it did not abolish it. The demand for commercial sex was simply driven underground, and its continuing presence manifested itself through another unmentionable subject, venereal disease. In 1913 the argument about prostitution and venereal disease, which is a constant theme throughout the 'long' century of debate reviewed here, was given added force when the suffragette Christabel Pankhurst wrote her pamphlet *The Great Scourge and how to end it*. In this she argued forcibly that respectable silence over prostitution and venereal disease was pure hypocrisy, since the men who refused to discuss the issue with their wives frequently had no compunction about using prostitutes, contracting the disease, and passing it on to their unsuspecting partners.

Pankhurst's pamphlet finally broke the popular taboo on discussing these issues. The debate in the 'long' nineteenth century had been conducted among intelligent, highly literate experts with access to a wide range of data, but had rarely penetrated into popular discourse. The 1913 Royal Commission into Venereal Disease, the parallel debates about national degeneracy which emerged in the *fin de siècle* climate, and above all the First World War with its necessity for mass education of troops in the dangers of using prostitutes, took public debate on prostitution into a new era.

My view is that the period from the 1790s to the First World War produced a distinct discourse on female prostitution. This discourse was characterised by moralism, earnestness and overt politics. It was often highly charged and emotional, but it was always fiercely argued and obsessed with facts – however dubious. It is recognisably a debate from the era of the Blue Books and painstaking empirical investigations into social phenomena. This was a time when intelligent people acted as if facts by themselves could decide complex moral issues. This view was mistaken, but it has left historians with an invaluable store of material to explore.

The sampling of this material offered in the following pages provides a unique insight into an aspect of life in nineteenth-century Britain which the inhabitants themselves often ignored, but which they found could not easily be rendered invisible. The issue being debated was whether society should tolerate prostitution as an inevitable phenomenon that should be regulated in the public interest – the

A scene from 'The Rake's Progress' by Hogarth. (Mary Evans Picture Library)

public health position – or suppressed as an intolerable evil – the moral purity position. The Victorians ended up supporting the puritans against the regulators, for the reasons which are set out here.

And yet prostitution did not go away. The echoes of the nineteenth-century debate are with us still. Perhaps by studying the manner in which the Victorians tried to resolve the debate between allowing prostitutes to ply their trade, or allowing puritans to seek to repress them, we can begin to understand better some of our own pressing political dilemmas over prostitution.

1   Parliamentary Debates (Hansard), 3rd Series, vol. 147, col. 853, 31 July 1857.
2   Parliamentary Papers 1881, House of Commons Paper no. 448 in vol. 9, printed 25 August 1881, Evidence of Howard Vincent, 19 July 1881.
3   Evidence of Howard Vincent, *op cit*, p. 64.

Prologue: Vice before Victoria

Female prostitution was endemic in the towns of pre-Victorian Britain. The Regency period and the reigns of George IV and William IV were notoriously scandalous, but also saw the rise of an increasingly vocal anti-vice lobby. This lobby scrutinised the vice-ridden towns of nineteenth-century Britain with outrage. It focused its attention on the capital, the largest and the most notorious urban area in the country. London was some ten times larger than even the fastest growing of the new industrial towns, and fascinated observers across a wide spectrum of interests.

The eyewitness testimonies selected here demonstrate not just the widespread existence of prostitution in Regency London, but the horrified fascination that

A scene from Hogarth's 'Harlot's Progress': a procuress and her victim. (Mansell Collection)

London vice created among those who observed it critically. Blake offers a modern sense of outrage against venereal disease, while the German Pückler Muskau and Frenchwoman Flora Tristan write of their amazement that the notoriously prudish British should tolerate prostitution on a vast scale.

Patrick Colquhoun's comments are, however, the most significant. His discussion of the lack of police powers was the opening salvo in a long-running campaign. In 1881 Howard Vincent would be saying much the same thing to a House of Lords select committee. Colquhoun sets out many of the key themes of the nineteenth-century debate, notably the inevitability of prostitution, which he argues justifies severe police powers. He also accepts Hogarth's 'Harlot's Progress' view of the career of the prostitute, and notoriously provides the first pseudo-figure for the number of prostitutes in the capital. Colquhoun's pamphlet was first published in 1796. By 1800 it had gone through six editions.

[Author's note: eio indicates emphasis in original.]

'London': William Blake, Songs of Experience, *1794*

I wander thro' each charter'd street,
Near where the charter'd Thames does flow,
And mark in every face I meet
Marks of weakness, marks of woe.

In every cry of every Man
In every Infant's cry of fear,
In every voice, in every ban,
The mind-forg'd manacles I hear.

How the Chimney-sweeper's cry
Every black'ning Church appalls;
And the hapless Soldier's sigh
Runs in blood down Palace walls.

But most thro' midnight streets I hear
How the youthful Harlot's curse
Blasts the new born Infant's tear,
And blights with plagues the Marriage hearse.

A Treatise on the Police of the Metropolis, *Patrick Colquhoun, 1800*

Chapter VII: Female Prostitution

In addition to the prominent causes, which contribute to the origin and the increase of crimes, which have been developed in the preceding Chapter, there are other sources still to be traced, from which infinite evils to the Community spring.

Among these the most important is, the state and condition of those unhappy females, who support themselves by Prostitution in this great Metropolis.

In contemplating their case, it is impossible to avoid dropping a tear of pity – Many of them perhaps originally seduced from a state of innocence, while they were the joy and comfort of their unhappy parents. Many of them born and educated to expect a better fate, until deceived by falsehood and villainy, they see their error when it is too late to recede. In this situation, abandoned by their relations and friends; deserted by their seducers, and at large upon the world . . . what are they to do? In the present unhappy state of things they seem to have no alternative, but to become the miserable instruments of promoting and practising that species of seduction and immorality, of which they themselves were the victims . . .

Thus it is from the multitudes of those unhappy Females, that assemble now in all parts of the town, that the morals of the youth are corrupted . . . Through this medium, APPRENTICES, CLERKS AND OTHER PERSONS IN TRUST [eio] are seduced from the paths of honesty – Masters are plundered, and Parents afflicted; while many a youth, who might have become the pride of his family – a comfort to the declining years of his parents, and an ornament to Society, exchanges a life of Virtue and Industry, for the pursuits of the Gambler, the Swindler and the Vagabond. Nor is the lot of these poor deluded females any less deplorable. Although a few of them may obtain settlements, while others bask for a while in the temporary sun-shine of ease and splendour, the major part end a short life in misery and wretchedness. . . .

Exposed to the rude insults of the inebriated and the vulgar; – the impositions of brutal officers and watchmen, and to the chilling blasts of the night, during the most inclement weather, in thin apparel . . . diseases, where their unhappy vocation does not produce them, are generated . . . till at length turned out into the streets, she languishes and ends her miserable days in an hospital or a workhouse, or perhaps perishes in some inhospitable hovel alone, without a friend to console her, or a fellow-mortal to close her eyes in the pangs of dissolution. . . .

To prevent its existence, even to a considerable extent, in so great a

Metropolis as London, is as impossible as to resist the torrent of the tides. It is an evil which must be endured while human passions exist; but it is at the same time an evil which may not only be lessened, but rendered less noxious and dangerous to the peace and good order of society; it may be stript of its indecency, and also of a considerable portion of the danger attached to it, to the youth of both sexes.

The lures for the seduction of youth passing along the streets in the course of their ordinary business, may be prevented by a Police, applicable to this subject, without either infringing upon the feelings of humanity or insulting distress; and still more is it practicable to remove the noxious irregularities, which are occasioned by the indiscreet conduct, and the shocking behaviour of Women of the Town . . . rendering the situation of modest women at once irksome and unsafe, either in places of public entertainment, or while passing along the most public streets of the Metropolis, particularly in the evening.

This unrestrained licence given to males and females, in the Walks of

An English prostitute of 1796 haggling.
(Mary Evans Picture Library)

Prostitution, was not known in former times at places of public resort, where there was at least an affectation of decency. To the disgrace, however, of the Police the evil has been suffered to increase; and the Boxes of Theatres often exhibit scenes, which are certainly extremely offensive to modesty, and contrary to that decorum to which the respectable part of the Community are entitled, when their families, often composed of young females, visit places of public resort . . .

For the purpose of understanding more clearly, by what means it is possible to lessen the evils arising from Female Prostitution in the Metropolis, it may be necessary to view it in all its ramifications. In point of extent it certainly exceeds credibility; but although there are many exceptions – the great mass (whatever their exterior may be), are mostly composed of women who have been in a state of menial servitude, and of whom not a few, from the love of idleness, with (in this case) the misfortune of good looks, have partly from inclination, not seldom from previous seduction and loss of character, resorted to Prostitution as a livelihood . . .

The whole may be estimated as follows:

1 Of the class of Well Educated women, it is earnestly hoped the number does not exceed	2,000
2 Of the class composed of persons above the rank of Menial Servants perhaps	3,000
3 Of the class who may have been employed as Menial Servants, or seduced in very early life, it is conjectured in all parts of the town, including Wapping, and the streets adjoining the River, there may be not less, who live wholly by prostitution, than	20,000
4 Of those in different ranks in Society, who live partly by prostitution, including the multitudes of low females, who cohabit with labourers and others without matrimony, there may be in all, in the Metropolis, about	25,000
Total	50,000

[Author's note: Colquhoun gives absolutely no grounds for these figures.]

When a general survey is taken of the Metropolis – the great numbers among the higher and middle classes of life who live unmarried – the multitudes of young men arriving at the age of puberty – the strangers who resort to the

Metropolis – The seamen and nautical labourers employed in the Trade of the River Thames, who amount to at least 40,000 – And the profligate state of Society in vulgar life, the intelligent mind will soon be reconciled to the statement, which at first view would seem to excite doubts, and require investigation.

But whether the numbers of these truly unfortunate women are a few thousands less or more is of no consequence in the present discussion, since it is beyond all doubt, that the evil is of a magnitude that is excessive, and imperiously calls for a remedy. – Not certainly a remedy against the possibility of Female Prostitution, for it has already been stated, that it is a misfortune which must be endured in large societies – All that can be attempted is, to divest it of the faculty of extending its noxious influence beyond certain bounds, and restrain those excesses and indecencies which have already been shown to be so extremely noxious to society, and unavoidably productive of depravity and crimes . . .

The evil is such as must be endured to a certain extent – because by no human power can it be overcome; but it can certainly be much diminished – perhaps only in one way – namely by prescribing rules – 'Thus far shall you go, and no further' – the rules of decorum shall be strictly preserved in the streets and in public places. In such situations Women of the Town shall no longer become instruments of seduction and debauchery . . . the example of Holland may be quoted, where, under its former Government, the morals of the people in general were supposed the purest of any in Europe, while the Police system was considered as among the best. Italy has also long shown an example, where Prostitutes were actually Licensed, with a view to secure Chastity against the inroads of violence, and to prevent the Public eye from being insulted by scenes of lewdness and indecorum . . .

Colquhoun made few clear proposals, either on police powers to sweep the streets or the licensing of prostitutes, but the thrust of his proposals is clear: regulation and police control. His pamphlet made an immediate impact and MPs called on him as an expert witness before the select committee of 1816 on the Police of the Metropolis. The following extract gives the concluding section of Colquhoun's evidence.

Report from The Times, *4 September 1816*

'You think that at present the law does not give sufficient power to touch the greater proportion of houses of ill fame?'

The law, I think, at present is defective as to those houses; they can only be touched by an indictment; it is very difficult to prove what they call 'bawdry' and they are generally convicted on the proof of their being disorderly houses; if there was summary jurisdiction, I think it would be much more effectual . . .

'You have mentioned that you thought it would be advantageous to proceed against houses by summary conviction; in what way would you suggest that the proceeding should take place?'

By summary convictions, with a power to inflict smaller penalties or a shorter imprisonment, the law would reach a vast number of persons keeping disorderly houses, which it is impossible to do in the circuitous and expensive mode of indictment.

'Is not the law defeated by the difficulty of obtaining the names of proprietors of houses of ill fame?'

There is a very great difficulty in prosecutions of this nature; although the offence is notorious, it must be proved that the occupier of the house pays the taxes; there are a variety of other legal niceties; and these people or their advisors are adepts in all of them . . .

'Do you think persons of feigned names are given in as the proprietors of those houses?'

Every trick that it is possible for the wit of man to devise is resorted to for the purpose of defeating the law in cases of this sort.

'Do you think that the difficulty in prosecuting with effect the proprietors of houses of ill fame deters many persons from attempting it?'

Although the prosecutions may be carried on by the parishes upon the requisitions of two housekeepers, it seldom happens that individuals trouble their heads about it, except where they are particularly annoyed by the nuisance.

'Are parishes deterred from prosecuting, in many cases, on account of the difficulty of conviction?'

The parishes must prosecute if two housekeepers will require the constable to do so; but the prosecutions are certainly less frequent than the evil to be remedied requires.

'Are prosecutions frequently defeated by the artifices of the keepers of those houses?'

Unless in very notorious cases, they are . . .

'Have you thought of any plan for the summary conviction of keepers of houses of ill fame?'

I should conceive that *the mere evidence of the persons residing in the house*, whether they paid the taxes or not, *and that they carried on a disorderly house*, for lodging prostitutes, *should be sufficient*; and that upon that proof alone they might be convicted; provided the penalty was moderate, and the imprisonment short. . . .

'Should you think that the evidence of two respectable housekeepers proving a disorderly house should prove sufficient to convict?

I certainly do.

'What in your opinion should constitute a disorderly house?'

The evidence of men entering a house with women known to be common prostitutes; and the general character of the house being proved to be a house of evil fame by the neighbours should be considered as sufficient evidence to obtain a conviction in a summary way . . .

'It is a well known fact, that *in no other capital in the world* is there the same outrageous behaviour on the part of prostitutes infesting the streets, which there is in this city; have you ever thought of any means by which that great evil might be checked?'

I have turned my attention to this excessive evil many times. I certainly think that, as the laws now stand, it is not possible to do much towards the diminution of this mass of profligacy and delinquency; and I am sorry to say it appears to increase, not only in the metropolis, but in all the principal towns in the kingdom . . .

'Would it be difficult, by directions given to the existing watchmen and patrols . . . to prevent the misbehaviour of the prostitutes in the street . . . in holding the language that they do, and seizing people as they do?'

It is not understood, according to law, that a watchman can seize a prostitute, unless she is in some shape disorderly; if she is riotous, drunk, or disturbing the neighbourhood . . .

'Have you thought of any plan for removing prostitutes from the streets?'

I have been consulted upon that subject by various respectable people residing in streets where they are much annoyed by the clamour of the disorderly prostitutes; and it occurred to me, that if any asylum were established in each parish, where all women known to be prostitutes could be sent by an order and under the authority of magistrates, after full examination, and ascertaining that they were living by prostitution alone, that means might be found through that medium, and by the means of religious and moral instruction, and introducing labour, to produce a reform. . . .

The Times *editorial comment on Colquhoun's evidence, 4 September 1816*

As Christians and Englishmen, our readers must blush to hear, that 'in no other capital in the world is there the same outrageous behaviour on the part of prostitutes infesting the streets, which there is in this city'. The fact is, however, incontrovertible. Paris is not to be compared with it; and much as we dislike French manners and French morals, we must candidly admit, from our own observations, that there is much less open and offensive vice in that city than in the British metropolis . . .

We think that very great good might be effected by some such measure as Dr Colquhoun recommends; namely, by establishing asylums, which should be 'supported partly by the labour of the females so far as it would go, and partly by the respective parishes and, perhaps, that they should have some assistance from the general revenues of the state'. Every person of the least experience must know that many of these unhappy women are obliged to continue in a state of profligacy and crime merely because they cannot obtain work to support themselves honestly; they have lost their character, and who will employ a prostitute from the streets . . . It is really farcical with me sometimes, when I have heard magistrates say, 'Young man, really I am very sorry for you; you are much to be pitied; you should turn your talents to a better account.' Yes, that is better said than done, for where is there any body to take these wretches? I will take it upon myself to say, that I have known this to be a clear case, which they have said to me, 'Sir, we do not thieve from disposition, but we thieve because we cannot get employment: our character is damned, and nobody will have us'; and so it is; there is no question about it.

In these proposed asylums, means might be found to reform these unhappy women, and in the mean time they would contribute greatly to their own support . . . We see no reason, however, why the respective parishes to which these women may belong should not contribute in some degree to their support in these asylums; it would make each parish more vigilant to repress the evil; and as to some assistance from the general revenues of the state, we think the money would be much better applied than in throwing it away in pensions, for which no services have been performed, and in sinecures, which hang like a millstone around the necks of the people. . . . it would be more honourable and glorious for this government to appropriate a few thousands annually for the reformation of public morals, and to endeavour to make this country as great in virtue as it is powerful in strength. At all events, Dr Colquhoun's plan deserves consideration.

OBSERVATIONS FROM OVERSEAS

The German prince Pückler Muskau visited England in the 1820s and wrote voluminous letters to his ex-wife in which he described his experiences of England. The letters have been published as *Pückler's Progress*, translated by Flora Brennan (Collins, 1987). The following extracts are taken from this book.

23rd November 1826 (pp. 49–50)
The striking thing to a foreigner in the local theatres here is the unheard of roughness and coarseness of the audience. It means that, apart from the Italian opera where only the best society congregates, the higher classes rarely visit their national theatre . . . A second reason for the absence of decent families from the theatre is the attendance of several thousand *filles de joie*, from the kept lady who devours six thousand sterling a year and has her own box, down to those who bivouac on the streets under the open sky. During the intermissions they crowd the large and fairly elaborate foyer, where they put all their effrontery unrestrainedly on show. It is strange that such spectacles are in no country on earth more shamelessly displayed than in pious and decent England. It goes on to such an extent that often in the theatre one can hardly ward off these repellent priestesses of Venus, especially when they are drunk, which is not infrequently the case, at which time they also beg in the most shameless fashion; one frequently sees the prettiest and best dressed young girl, who does not disdain to accept a shilling or sixpence just like the lowest beggar woman, getting herself half a glass of rum or ginger beer at the bar – and such things go on, I repeat, in the national theatre of the English, where their highest dramatic talent is displayed; where immortal artists, like Garrick, Mrs Siddons, Miss O'Neil enchanted by their excellence, and where today's heroes such as Kean, Kemble and Young make their appearance! . . .

The Ambassador of — accompanied me to the theatre and told me . . . many not uninteresting details concerning this or that beauty as she swept by . . . 'That one with the languishing eyes', said he, 'has just come out of the King's Bench, where she has been for a year because of £8,000 worth of debts, still practising her profession though and, God knows how, finally finding the means of getting free. She has a strange weakness for her station in life, to wit, sentimentality, and has been known to give a lover ten times more than she receives from her protector . . .

'See that rather overblown beauty,' he went on. 'Ten years ago she was living on a scale of luxury which few of my colleagues could emulate. Far from laying by part of her riches of those days, she had a real passion for throwing everything out of the window, and today she will be grateful if you help her with a shilling.'

In contrast to these poor things, he showed me later, in one of the best boxes, a charming woman of the highest standing who had married a man with an income of twenty thousand pounds, and yet was only too willing to be all things to all men for just one of those guineas.

Flora Tristan was a French socialist and feminist who visited London in 1826, 1831, 1835 and 1839. In 1840 she published *Promenades dans Londres*, a record of her 1839 visit, but also drawing on her previous visits. Her insights into upper, middle and working class attitudes to prostitution are particularly interesting as they come from an early feminist perspective. These extracts are taken from *The London Journal of Flora Tristan*, translated, annotated and introduced by Jean Hawkes from the 1842 edition and published by Virago in 1982.

The London Journal of Flora Tristan

pp. 83–7

There are so many prostitutes in London that one sees them everywhere at any time of day; all the streets are full of them, but at certain times they flock in from outlying districts in which most of them live, and mingle with the crowds in theatres and public places. It is rare for them to take men home; their landlords would object, and besides their lodgings are unfit. They take their 'captures' to the houses reserved for their trade . . .

Between seven and eight o'clock one evening, accompanied by two friends armed with canes, I went to take a look at the new suburb which lies on either side of the long broad thoroughfare called Waterloo Road at the end of Waterloo Bridge. This neighbourhood is almost entirely inhabited by prostitutes and people who live off prostitution; it is courting danger to go there alone at night. It was a hot summer evening; in every window and doorway women were laughing and joking with their protectors. Half dressed, some of them *naked to the waist* [eio], they were a revolting sight, and the criminal, cynical expressions of their companions filled me with apprehension. These men are for the most part very good looking – young, vigorous and well made – but their coarse and common air marks them as animals whose sole instinct is to satisfy their appetites . . .

We went on our way and explored all the streets in the vicinity of Waterloo Road, then we sat upon the bridge to watch the women of the neighbourhood flock past, as they do every night between the hours of eight and nine, on their way to the West End, where they ply their trade all through the night and return home between eight and nine in the morning. They infest the promenades and any other place where people gather, such as the approaches to the Stock Exchange, the various public buildings and the theatres,which they invade as soon as entry is reduced to half price . . . After the play they move on to the 'finishes'; these are squalid taverns or vast resplendent gin-palaces where people go to spend what remains of the night . . .

I had heard descriptions of the debauchery to be seen at finishes, but could never bring myself to believe them. Now I was in London for the fourth time with the firm resolve to discover everything for myself. I determined to overcome my repugnance and go in person to one of these finishes. . . . The same friends who had accompanied me to the Waterloo Road again offered to be my guides . . .

From the outside these 'gin-palaces' with their carefully fastened shutters seem to be quietly slumbering; but no sooner has the doorkeeper admitted you by the little door reserved for the initiates than you are dazzled by the light of a thousand gas lamps. Upstairs there is a spacious salon divided down the middle; in one half there is a row of tables separated one from the other by wooden screens, as in all English restaurants . . . In the other half there is a dais where the prostitutes parade in all their finery; seeking to arouse the men with their glances and remarks . . .

Towards midnight the regular clients begin to arrive; several finishes are frequented by men in high society, and this is where the cream of the aristocracy gather. At first the young noblemen recline on the sofas, smoking and exchanging pleasantries with the women; then, when they have drunk enough for the fumes of champagne and Madeira to go to their heads, the illustrious scions of the English nobility, the very honourable members of Parliament remove their coats, untie their cravats, take off their waistcoats and braces, and proceed to set up their private boudoir in a public place. Why not make themselves at home, since they are paying out so much money for the right to display their contempt . . . The orgy rises to a crescendo; between four and five o'clock in the morning it reaches its height.

Prostitutes dividing the spoils, 1796. (Ashton, *Old Times*. Mary Evans Picture Library)

At this point it takes a good deal of courage to remain in one's seat, a mute spectator of all that takes place. What a worthy use these English lords make of their immense fortunes! How fine and generous they are when they have lost the use of their reason and offer fifty, even a hundred guineas to a prostitute if she will lend herself to all the obscenities that drunkenness engenders . . .

For in a finish there is no lack of entertainment. One of the favourite sports is to *ply a woman with drink* until she falls dead drunk upon the floor, then to make her swallow a draught compounded of *vinegar, mustard and pepper*; this invariably throws the poor creature into horrible convulsions, and her spasms and contortions provoke the *honourable company* to gales of laughter and infinite amusement. Another diversion much appreciated at these fashionable gatherings is to empty the contents of the nearest glass upon the women as they lie insensible on the ground. I have seen satin dresses of no recognisable colour, only a confused mass of stains; wine, brandy, beer, tea, coffee, cream etc . . . daubed all over them in a thousand fantastic shapes . . . The air is heavy with the noxious odours of food, drink, tobacco, and others more fetid still which seize you by the throat, grip your temples in a vice and make your senses reel:

it is indescribably horrible! . . . However, this life, which continues relentlessly night after night, is the prostitute's sole hope of a fortune, for she has no hold on the Englishmen when he is sober. *The sober Englishman is chaste to the point of prudery.*

It is usually between seven and eight o'clock in the morning when people leave the finish. The servants go out to look for cabs, and anyone still on his feet gathers up his clothes and returns home; as for the rest, the pot-boys dress them in the first garments that come to hand, bundle them into a cab and tell the cabman where to deliver them. Often nobody knows their address; then they are deposited in the cellar and left to sleep in the straw. This place is known as the drunkards hole, and there they stay until they have recovered their wits sufficiently to say where they wish to be taken.

Discussing the prevalence of child prostitution, Flora Tristan quotes a document produced by the Society for the Prevention of Juvenile Prostitution in 1838. The Society had prosecuted a brothel specialising in the prostitution of young girls, mostly foreign. This caused the madam, a Frenchwoman named Marie Aubrey, to fly abroad to escape imprisonment.

pp. 96–7

The house in question was situated in Seymour Place, Bryanston Square. It was an establishment of great notoriety, visited by some of the most distinguished foreigners and others . . . The house consisted of twelve or fourteen rooms, besides those appropriated to domestic uses, each of which was genteely and fashionably furnished . . . a service of solid silver plate was ordinarily in use when the visitors required it, which was the property of Marie Aubrey. At the time the prosecution was instituted, there were about twelve or fourteen young females in the house, mostly from France and Italy . . . Marie Aubrey had lived in the house a number of years, and had amassed a fortune . . . Upon receiving a fresh importation of females, it was the practice of this woman to send a circular, stating the circumstance, to the parties who were in the habit of visiting the establishment . . .

There are a number of houses of this description at [sic] the West End now under the cognizance of the Society, and whose circulars are in its possession, who adopt this plan, and by means of the Court Guide and twopenny post, are forwarding notices of their establishments indiscriminately to all.

'Your Committee desire to lay before this meeting the means adopted by the agents of these houses. As soon as they arrive on the Continent they obtain information respecting those families who have daughters, and who are desirous of placing them in respectable situations; they then introduce themselves, and by fair promise induce the parents to allow the stranger to accompany the stranger to London, with the understanding that they are to be engaged as tambour workers, or in some other genteel occupation . . . While they remain in the house they were first taken to, the money is duly forwarded, and their parents are thus unconsciously receiving the means of support from the prostitution of their own children; if they remove, letters are sent to the parents to apprize them that their daughters have left the employ of their former mistress, and the money is accordingly stopped.'

Flora Tristan also provides the following revealing story:

While I was in London, a city merchant who was suffering from a bad disease imagined that he had contracted it from a prostitute of his acquaintance; he arranged to meet her at a house of assignation, where he tied her skirts above her head so that from the waist upward she was confined in a sort of sack; then he beat her with a birch-rod until he was worn out, and finally threw her out into the street just as she was. The wretched woman was suffocating for want of air; she struggled, shouted and rolled about in the mud, but nobody came to her aid. In London people never interfere in what happens in the street: 'That is not my business', an Englishman will say, without even stopping, and he is already ten paces off by the time his words reach your ears. The poor woman lying on the pavement was no longer moving and would have died had not a policeman come and cut the string which tied her clothes. Her face was purple and she was hardly breathing, she was asphyxiated. She was taken to hospital where prompt treatment restored her to life.

    The man responsible for this abominable assault was summoned before the magistrate and was fined six shillings for offending against morality on the public highway.

    In a nation so ridiculously prudish, the penalty for outraging public decency is clearly not very high . . . but what is surprising is that the magistrate saw nothing in this act but a misdemeanour and judged it accordingly . . .

Part One: The Puritan Offensive, 1835–1850

----

1. Puritan Polemics, 1835–1841

The 1830s were a time of political and social ferment in Britain. The Industrial Revolution had brought into being new social groups, which struggled to exert themselves politically and culturally. The urban middle classes succeeded in gaining the vote in 1832, forcing the disenfranchised working class to turn to Chartism. Political challenges to the aristocratic order added point to existing criticisms of the moral laxity of the Regency period, and may have contributed to a sharpening debate on prostitution. The coming to the throne of the eighteen-year-old Queen Victoria in 1837 may have made a psychological difference as well, though the major triumph of Victorian values in the field of prostitution was not to happen till the 1880s.

Whatever the reasons, puritan investigation and agitation about female prostitution intensified in the late 1830s and continued through the 1840s. This initial puritan offensive failed to make an impact because it was unable to mobilise enough political mass to outweigh the intransigence of the male political elite. Its supporters were too easily dismissed as ineffective do-gooders or politically marginal individuals. It attracted no major political figures, no major journalists, and no charismatic public campaigners capable of winning mass support. The contrast with the movement after 1870, led by James Stansfeld and Josephine Butler and attracting the support of W.T. Stead and the *Pall Mall Gazette* at the critical moment, is very marked.

The anti-vice movement of the 1830s and 1840s certainly showed the willingness of a militant minority to investigate prostitution despite the restrictions of a prudish society. Its supporters were, however, insubstantial figures whose research was often defective and who too often substituted rhetoric for solid evidence. A group of earnest thinkers and investigators including the Congregationalist ministers William Bevan and Robert Vaughn, physicians William Tait and Michael Ryan, and puritan reformers William Logan and John Talbot investigated prostitution but lacked the skills to jolt the public out of its deeply rooted indifference. The extracts given here from pamphlets by Michael Ryan and William Tait illustrate the weaknesses of the puritan approach at this time, as the effective critique by Ralph Wardlaw shows.

These weaknesses are particularly clear in the work of Michael Ryan. His survey of prostitution in the capital was based largely on the work of the deeply puritanical London Rescue Society and its secretary, J.B. Talbot. The estimated figure of 80,000 prostitutes in London, asserted by the Society and quoted by Ryan without a shred of evidence, became deeply engrained in puritan folklore and was still resurfacing in the early twentieth century. Tait was less rhetorical but was still prepared to use Colquhoun's suspect figures in his own argument.

Dr Michael Ryan published *Prostitution in London* in 1839, using the reports of the London Society for the Protection of Young Females and Prevention of Juvenile Prostitution. The first extract quotes directly from the Society's founding document, published in May 1835, and gives a distinct flavour of the sermonising approach which alienated all but the most fervently committed. Ryan is, however, on stronger ground when referring – accurately – to the inadequacy of the law against brothels. He states eloquently the puritan case for a strengthening of the law against brothels, a call which was to fall on stony ground for another forty-five years.

Prostitution in London, *pp. 118–21*
The Committee cannot avoid referring to the present dreadfully immoral state of the British Metropolis. No one can pass through the streets of London without being struck with the awfully depraved condition of a certain class of the youth of both sexes at this period. Nor is it too much to say, that in London crime has arrived at a frightful magnitude; nay, it is asserted, that nowhere does it exist to such an extent as in this highly favoured city. . . .

A long catalogue of crimes peculiar to the metropolis might be enumerated; suffice it, after what has been stated, to direct the attention of the public to the abominable system of traffic carried on by the traders in Juvenile Prostitution. It has been proved that upwards of four hundred individuals procure a livelihood by trepanning females from eleven to fifteen years of age, for the purposes of Prostitution. Every art is practised, every scheme devised to effect this object; and when an innocent child appears in the streets without a protector, she is insidiously watched by one of these merciless wretches and decoyed, under some plausible pretext, to an abode of infamy and degradation. No sooner is the unsuspecting helpless one within their grasp, than, by a preconcerted measure, she becomes a victim to their inhuman designs. She is stripped of the apparel with which parental care, or friendly solicitude had clothed her, and then, decked with the gaudy trappings of her shame, she is compelled to walk the streets . . .

With regret it is stated, that the instances of Juvenile Prostitution are exceedingly numerous, and most of them take place in the manner just depicted. Not less than 80,000 Prostitutes exist in London – a great proportion of whom are of tender age. It is computed that 8,000 die every year, and yet the number so far from being reduced, is rather on the increase – the market, as it were, being constantly supplied by those who are ever on the alert to entrap the

PROSTITUTION IN LONDON,

WITH A

COMPARATIVE VIEW

OF THAT OF

PARIS AND NEW YORK,

AS ILLUSTRATIVE OF THE CAPITALS AND LARGE TOWNS OF
ALL COUNTRIES; AND PROVING MORAL   DEPRAVATION
TO BE THE MOST FERTILE SOURCE OF CRIME,
AND OF PERSONAL AND SOCIAL MISERY;

WITH

AN ACCOUNT OF THE NATURE AND TREATMENT OF THE VARIOUS
DISEASES, CAUSED BY THE ABUSES OF THE
REPRODUCTIVE FUNCTION.

ILLUSTRATED BY NUMEROUS PLATES.

BY MICHAEL RYAN, M.D.,

MEMBER OF THE ROYAL COLLEGES OF PHYSICIANS AND SURGEONS IN LONDON,
SENIOR PHYSICIAN TO THE METROPOLITAN FREE HOSPITAL,
LECTURER ON THE PRACTICE OF MEDICINE, ETC.

LONDON:

H. BAILLIERE, 219, REGENT STREET.

PARIS: J. B. BAILLIERE, RUE DE L'ECOLE DE MEDECINE.
LEIPSIG: J. A. G. WEIGEL.

MDCCCXXXIX

The title page of Michael Ryan's *Prostitution in London*, 1839. (Author
Collection)

London prostitutes of 1841. (*Snell's Guide to the Metropolis*. Mary Evans Picture Library)

innocent and the unwary. Here then is an amount of human misery, arising from one source! Nature is thus outraged, and the noblest powers of our species debased to the level of the brute. Incalculable is the suffering thus inflicted upon these unfortunate creatures – Incalculable is the mischief forced upon society, by the example here produced.

The trusting Dr Ryan proceeded to display absolute belief in the figure of 80,000 prostitutes offered by the Society. This figure had been devised by the Society's secretary, Mr Talbot, without any effective evidence.

pp. 168–9

Mr Talbot concludes, after the most laborious research and personal observation, and the evidence of eight different investigators, that there are 80,000 prostitutes in London. He gives the comparative state of the population and licentiousness in Norwich, Belfast, Liverpool and London, by which it appears that the number in the latter would be 52,000. But as crime has increased three or four hundred per cent during the last twenty years, while the population did not advance more than thirty three per cent, the inference is, that licentiousness, as well as other vices, extends in a tenfold ratio. He conscientiously believes, there is no exaggeration in the number he has given . . .

Some writers maintain, that every one in three of the daughters of persons in the lower rank in life, become prostitutes, before they are twenty years of age. It is also asserted, that there is one prostitute to every seven virtuous women. . . .

Penitentiaries may rescue the fallen, but the only power on earth that will reach the brothel-keeper, and restrain him, is the law. If the brothel-keeper and his agents are brought under severe and effective enactments, it will follow that the number of prostitutes must be reduced, and consequently every other crime, in a proportionate ratio, lessened. If this be true, and I doubt not it will be admitted, the inquiry will naturally be made, 'What laws are there already in existence, and how far are they calculated to effect the desired end?'

Several legislative enactments have been passed, viz. 25 Geo. II, c.36, 28 Geo. II, c.19, and 58 Geo. III, c.70. Neither of these acts is at all sufficient to reach the evil; nevertheless much good may be done by their being vigorously enforced by the proper authorities, which are the officers of the parishes . . . The first of these enactments is, indeed, the only one under which brothel-keepers can be indicted . . . much difficulty attends the administration of this act, independent of the culpable neglect of parish officers . . . The 36 Geo. II provides that when any two ratepayers of any given parish, give notice in writing to the constables or overseers of the said parish, of the existence of a brothel in such a parish, that it shall be the duty of the said officers to accompany the said two inhabitants to a justice of the peace . . . upon this the magistrate is to issue his warrant for the apprehension of the accused, and the two inhabitants are again to appear before the justice, and the man or woman is held to bail to answer the charge at the sessions, where the two inhabitants must attend to give or produce the material evidence; and if a conviction is obtained, the two inhabitants may claim a reward of £10, but if the prosecution fails, they are liable to an action. The parish ought to pay all the expenses of the prosecution of the brothel-keeper . . . It should be known, also, that material evidence is the production of a witness who has had criminal intercourse in the house. No respectable individual would adopt this course himself, and every virtuous mind must entertain a repugnance to making a witness guilty, or even producing a guilty person to give evidence. These circumstances render the act inoperative, and it is rarely acted upon . . .

I would suggest that an Act of Parliament should be passed, founded upon the principle of summary jurisdiction, with an extension of the powers of the police and magistracy, giving to any person, whether parishioner or not, the right to complain to a magistrate of the existence of a brothel; and that the evidence of the police or the neighbours should be sufficient, without requiring a guilty witness to be produced, to authorise the magistrate to send the accused to prison for any term not exceeding six months; reserving to himself the right, in the event of a very flagrant case, to commit the offending party to trial as a felon. All the expenses to be paid by the country as in cases of felony . . . A system of harassing might thus be kept up, the cases would obtain publicity in the police reports, the number of brothels be reduced, and deeds of infamy soon be suppressed . . .

As evidence, Ryan's pamplet was weak, and the lack of hard fact and use of overheated language did the puritan cause no good at all. However, Ryan's discussion, and the work of the London Rescue Society on which he drew, sparked similar investigations and debates in other towns. One of the most persuasive of the puritan tracts produced in the immediate aftermath of Ryan's publication was *Magdalenism: an Inquiry into the Extent, Causes and Consequences of Prostitution in Edinburgh*, which was published in 1840 by William Tait. A member of the Anatomical Society, Tait was formerly House Surgeon to the Edinburgh Lock Hospital, where he had gained professional experience of working with prostitutes. His assessment of the difficulties in estimating the numbers of prostitutes shows more sophistication than Ryan could muster, but overall relied heavily on supposition.

Tait's pamphlet consciously reinforced Ryan's call for a tightening of the law. Tait called for police action to clear the streets of prostitutes, and to suppress brothels. The

MAGDALENISM.

AN INQUIRY

INTO THE

EXTENT, CAUSES, AND CONSEQUENCES.

OF

PROSTITUTION IN EDINBURGH.

By WILLIAM TAIT, SURGEON,

MEMBER OF THE ANATOMICAL SOCIETY, AND OF THE PHRENOLOGICAL
ASSOCIATION ; FORMERLY HOUSE SURGEON TO THE EDINBURGH LOCK
HOSPITAL, AND SURGEON TO THE MIDWIFERY DISPENSARY,
HIGH SCHOOL YARDS, EDINBURGH.

SECOND EDITION.

EDINBURGH: P. RICKARD, SOUTH BRIDGE

GEORGE GALLIE AND JOHN M'LEOD, GLASGOW ;
AND S. HIGHLY, LONDON.

MDCCCXLII.

The title page of William Tait's *Magdalenism. An Inquiry into the Extent, Causes and Consequences of Prostitution in Edinburgh*, 1842. (Author Collection)

1842 edition, however, was no simple call for repression. Tait wanted the prostitutes reclaimed via Magdalene Asylums. He hoped that 'No relaxation on the part of the public mind will take place till a complete change, both in relation to the suppression of the crime of prostitution itself and the protection of its victims, shall have been been accomplished.' His even-handed approach to suppression and reclamation was not taken up by the puritan mainstream. While much effort was to be devoted to the rescue of prostitutes, where state action was concerned the thrust of the puritan campaign was entirely on suppression, with reclamation left to unsystematic private activity. Tait's thrust toward repression is therefore focused on in the following extracts from *Magdalenism*, 1842.

Magdalenism: an Inquiry into . . . Prostitution in Edinburgh, 1842

Number of Prostitutes in Edinburgh, pp. 5–8

Inquiry has been made in various quarters where information was expected to be obtained on this point, but the answers received are so vague and unsatisfactory that no reliance can be placed on them. One individual estimated the number of prostitutes at 6,000, and another so low as 300 . . . Captain Stuart, late of the Police Establishment, who is the best authority on all subjects relating to blackguards of all description, confessed that he could give no opinion on the subject. . . .

The method which has been adopted in the present inquiry has been to ascertain, first, the number of brothels in the city, and then the number of girls kept in each . . . The number of houses of bad fame, including houses of assignation, licensed taverns, and eating houses where sexual intercourse is tolerated, amounts to about two hundred. The average number of girls who board and lodge in these houses, independent of those who occasionally sleep there, or visit them with their cowlies [clients], is about three to each, making the number necessary for the supply of these dens of vice about six hundred – the number in private lodgings, in rooms of their own, or living with friends, is about two hundred; amounting to about 800, or one to every eighty of the adult male population . . .

The number already given is taken from those who not only appear publicly on the streets, but who accept of the addresses of all who present themselves to them, and therefore fall properly under the definition of Prostitute, which has been given elsewhere . . .

[Author's note: Tait gives no source for his figures.]

Probable Number of Sly Prostitutes in Edinburgh, pp. 8–11

This is a question of considerable difficulty and uncertainty, arising from the impossibility of ascertaining the number of those who live partly on the wages of prostitution, but are ostensibly of fair character. There can be little doubt, however, that secret prostitution prevails to a very alarming extent . . . It may be considered uncharitable to suppose, what may nevertheless be confidently asserted as a fact, that about one third of those girls engaged in sedentary occupations, at one time or another deliver themselves up to this wicked life. Some, it is true, are more prone to it than others; and while some make it a regular habit, others do so only at certain periods, when they are either out of employment, or find their scanty earnings inadequate to gratify their ambition for fine dress; and the greater part of them may be more discriminate in the selection of those they admit into their company than common prostitutes are, though in other respects they are equally abandoned.

Suppose, then, that there are 2,000 females engaged in sedentary employment, a third part would give a little more than 660 sly prostitutes belonging to this particular class; add to this 300 servant girls, which is the lowest calculation that can be made, and 200 women who are either widows or have been deserted by their husbands – and the number of sly prostitutes together will amount to 1,160 and upwards.

This calculation rests in a great measure on supposition; but were the truth precisely known, it would appear that there is no exaggeration, but the reverse . . . Out of 300 girls employed in sewing and book stitching, whose history has been ascertained, 130 are known to deliver themselves partially up to a life of prostitution. It follows, therefore, that if the whole of these particular classes of girls are immoral – and there is no ground to suppose that they are not – one third of the whole must be secretly prostitutes . . .

[Author's note: Tait fails to give any serious evidence for his allegations. Prosecutions and police action are not studied, and the evidence given is largely anecdotal. The central puritan weakness of lack of solid evidence is manifest.]

Prostitution amongst Servants and the Manner in which they Pursue it, pp. 11–13
Prostitution amongst servants is a very aggravated and unsuspected evil. Strangers, whose characters may be of the worst description, are consequently admitted into the houses of respectable families, where thefts, to a considerable extent, are not unfrequently committed. So many cases of this kind have come to the author's knowledge, that he considers it his duty to disclose to the public all that he knows of those criminal practices, and by this means put many on their guard who are unconsciously exposed to this evil. . . .

It has been observed, that there may be about 300 servants in Edinburgh who deliver themselves up more or less to a life of clandestine prostitution.

Three hundred families are thus at the mercy of unprincipled domestics, and are liable to have their property destroyed or carried off by individuals who have been admitted into their dwellings without their knowledge or consent . . .

The number of servants, however, who adopt this method, though in itself considerable, is small in comparison with the number of those who pursue the same wicked course by different means. More than three quarters of the servants addicted to this scandalous mode of living, have no opportunity of inviting their lovers to their masters' houses; and consequently, must either meet with them in the open air, or make appointments. . . .

Chapter Five: On the Means to be Adopted for the Suppression of Prostitution and for Reforming its Unfortunate Victims

Prostitutes must necessarily be banished from the public streets, pp. 294–302
Were prostitutes prevented from exercising their calling on the streets, the evil of prostitution would soon be greatly diminished; and no plan that may be introduced for the abolition of this evil will be attended with success, unless this object be kept specially in view . . .

The advantages to be derived from banishing prostitution from the streets, are both numerous and important. 'That a prudent and discreet regulation of prostitutes in this great metropolis,' observes Colquhoun, 'would operate powerfully, not only in gradually diminishing their numbers, but also in securing public morals against the insults to which they are exposed, both in the open streets and at places of public entertainment, cannot be denied. That young men in pursuit of their lawful business in the streets of this metropolis [London] would be secured against that ruin and infamy which temptations thus calculated to inflame the passions have brought upon many who would otherwise have passed through life as useful and respectable members of society, is equally true. . . .

'Were such proper regulations once adopted, the ears and eyes of the wives and daughters of the modest and unoffending citizens, who cannot afford to travel in carriages, would no longer be insulted by gross and polluted language, and great indecency of behaviour, while walking the streets . . .'

A proposal to prevent prostitutes from walking on the streets, might to many seem too illiberal and despotic for the present enlightened era. Why, it may be asked, prohibit these unfortunate creatures enjoying themselves in the open air as well as other citizens? To this there can be no objection whatever, provided their conduct, when they did come forth to public view, is such as to conceal their true character and calling. It is not as a punishment to them that such a measure is advocated, but for the safety of the morals of the community . . .

Necessity of the Interference of the Magistrates and Police Authorities, p. 303
It will be seen that the object alluded to in the preceding observations can only be attained by the assistance of the Magistrates and Police Authorities. On this subject there may be different opinions; and many objections may be urged against such an interference, as being beyond the pale of their authority, and an encroachment on the private rights of the citizens. What can rationally be opposed to this arrangement? Let Dr Colquhoun answer the question. 'Not surely religion, for it will tend to advance it; not morality, for the effect of the measure will increase and promote it; not that it will sanction and encourage what will prove offensive and noxious in society, since all that is noxious and offensive is by this arrangment to be removed. Where then lies the objection? *In vulgar prejudice only.* By those of inferior education, whose peculiar habits and pursuits have generated strong prejudices, this excuse may be pleaded; but by the intelligent and well informed, it will be viewed through a more correct medium' . . . [eio]

[Author's note: The puritans at this stage had very poor political skills.]

Magistrates ought to be Invested with Summary Powers to Suppress Houses of Bad Fame and to Convict and Punish Brothel-Keepers, Procuresses and Others Pandering to a Life of Prostitution, pp. 319–23
As there may be doubts regarding the powers which Magistrates at present possess, and as the evil of prostitution is of such a nature that no hope can be entertained of its suppression without the interference of the civil authorities, it is necessary that full authority be granted to them by Parliament to adopt every measure which they deem fit for obtaining so desirable an object. No person who has any wish for the welfare of the citizens, has the least doubt regarding the propriety of suppressing gambling-houses and other riotous places; yet it is somewhat surprising that the powers of the Magistrates have never been extended to the putting down of houses of bad fame. Is there any comparison between the evils resulting from a gambling house and those arising from the toleration of a public brothel? . . .

The following observations from the work of Dr Ryan are so striking and appropriate, that it is considered best to give them verbatim: 'Every thing which has even the appearance of evil should be at once suppressed. But this can only be effected by extending the powers of the Magistracy and Police, and after this, by a most rigid classification of persons committed to prison. . .'

Dr Ryan, after showing that the various legislative enactments that have been passed . . . are inadequate to reach the evil, as also the difficulties which attend their administration, suggests the total repeal of these Acts so far as regards brothels; and a more easy, simple and efficient method adopted in its place. 'I would suggest', says he, 'that an Act of Parliament should be passed, founded upon the principle of summary jurisdiction, with an extension of the powers of the police and magistracy, giving to any person the right to complain to a magistrate of the existence of a brothel; and that the evidence of the police and neighbours to the fact should be sufficient, without requiring a guilty witness to be produced, to authorise the magistrate to send the accused to prison for any term not exceeding six months . . .'

While brothel-keepers are permitted to continue unmolested, as they are at present, little permanent good can be expected. . . . They have resources at their command . . . their agents, the procuresses, are ramified throughout the whole city and suburbs, and are exerting all their energies to entrap the innocent and unsuspicious. If the source of this evil were attacked and destroyed, such diabolical proceedings would also be terminated. 'Every person', observes the author already so freely quoted under this head, 'found detected in using indecent incentives, or selling indecent publications, or in any way promoting and encouraging prostitution, or an illicit intercourse, should be punished as the brothel-keeper . . .'

Probably it would be conformable with sound policy to renew some of the ancient Acts of the Edinburgh town council, which punish the male as well as the female offenders. It is scarcely consistent with the principles of justice that the one sex should suffer solely for a crime of which the other is equally culpable . . .

Tait may have had abstract logic on his side, but these were hardly arguments calculated to convince an all-male legislature which could well be enacting punishments that could rebound on its own head. The statistical foundations of the puritan arguments were weak, and their political skills seriously deficient. Both were to be cruelly exposed, statistically by Dr Ralph Wardlaw and in the political arena by the fate of the 1844 Bill to suppress brothels proposed by the Bishop of Exeter.

2. Critics and Legislators: the Pamphlet War and Exeter's Bill of 1844

Colquhoun, Talbot, Ryan, Tait and the anti-vice lobby of which they were a part, were highly vocal by the early 1840s. That they did not yet speak for the mainstream of Victorian values became clear with the failure of Exeter's Bill against brothels in 1844. The political elite of mid-century Britain was immune to the tactics used by the puritan fringe, and dismissed their activities as the actions of an irrelevant minority. The dubious use of statistics by the puritans provided an easy target for critics, as demonstrated by this extract from *Lectures on Female Prostitution: its Nature, Extent, Guilt Causes and Remedy*, by Ralph Wardlaw DD, given in Glasgow in 1842.

Lectures on Female Prostitution, *Ralph Wardlaw*, 1842

On the important point of the *extent* to which, under its various forms, prostitution prevails in our own country, and especially in our principal cities and towns, it is an exceedingly difficult matter to arrive at any certainty; or even – judging from the disparity, in some instances, between the representations of different authorities – to make any satisfactory approach to the truth. In proof of this, I shall, first of all, present you with the following Extract from the Review of the work of Parent-Duchalet on the Prostitution of Paris, in the *Foreign Quarterly Review*, no. XXXVIII, July 1837, pages 340 and 341. 'The extent of prostitution is the first subject that engages our attention; and there is scarcely any example more striking, of the exaggerations that result from the neglect of statistical accuracy. There have been frequent guesses at the number of unfortunate beings engaged in it, both in Paris and London. In the former capital, it has been publicly stated, that the number exceeded sixty thousand; and they were accounted very moderate indeed who reduced the number to one half that amount; – but the registers of police, which have been very accurately kept for the last twenty years, prove that there were never so many as four thousand at one time engaged in this profligate course. Colquhoun's *Police of the Metropolis*, a work possessing more authority than it has any title to claim, estimates the number of prostitutes in London at fifty thousand: but the investigations instituted by Mr Mayne led to the conclusion that there are not more than from eight to ten thousand, and the smaller amount is more probable than the larger.

The mistake of the amount of prostitutes is so common, and so injurious, that we think it would be useful to indicate the sources of the error. The first of these is the fluctuating nature of this portion of the population. The superintendents of our metropolitan police have frequently noticed the rapidity and the suddenness with which many of those on whom they have kept a watchful eye disappear from the stage, leaving no trace by which their further progress could be followed. . . . A second cause of error is that persons estimate the amount for the entire city from the numbers found in certain localities; and this was the source of Colquhoun's enormous estimate.

Finally, we have been informed by some intelligent police officers, that the same persons haunt different parts of the metropolis at different hours, and are consequently counted many times over. It must, however, be confessed that there are no means for estimating the amount of depraved women in London, with anything like accuracy. The nearest approach we can make to it is that their number is not much more than double that of the same class in Paris.

Here, you will observe, we have, with regard to Paris, a range of estimate, from under *four* thousand to above *sixty* thousand – and with regard to London, the range of from *eight* thousand to *fifty* thousand is far from being the full extent of the differences: for, while the metropolitan police reckon the number of prostitutes at *seven* thousand, it has been stated by some – Mr Talbot, Dr Ryan, Dr Campbell, and others, so high as *eighty* thousand! Respecting the latter statement, which rises so far above even what the reviewer just cited calls Mr Colquhoun's 'enormous estimate', the following remarks, in the *London City Mission* magazine for November 1840, may suffice to show its extravagance: 'Dr Ryan has stated, in common with many others, that the number of females already alluded to is 80,000 – but he does so chiefly on the authority of Mr Talbot. In a report of the Society for the prevention of juvenile prostitution, and quoted by Dr Ryan, it is said, that "it has been ascertained that full two thirds of the unfortunate females in our streets are under twenty years of age". This gives us, out of the 80,000, upwards of 53,000 of this tender age. By the population returns of 1821, it appears that fifty out of every hundred of the population are under twenty years of age; and that one tenth of the whole population is between the ages of fifteen and twenty. The whole number of our female population between the ages of fifteen and twenty, according to the last census, is 78,962; and can it be true that 53,000 of them are prostitutes?'

And again, giving the result under another form; 'In the last population returns for London within and without the walls, Southwark, Westminster, the parishes within the bills of mortality, and adjacent parishes not within the bills (the extent of the Metropolis to which such a calculation would be confined), the number of males is given at 684,441, and of females at 789,628. By the population returns of 1821, it appears that of every 100 persons twenty are under seven years of age, twenty between the ages of seven and fifteen, and ten between fifteen and twenty, leaving fifty out of every hundred from the age of twenty and upward. If, therefore, we deduct, for female children under fifteen years of age, and for females above fifty, only one half of the female population, we have 394,814 females in reference to whom the calculation can be made. If we divide this number by 80,000, it gives us nearly *five*, and is it true, that one out of every five females in London, between the ages of fifteen and fifty, including the highest, the middling, and the humbler classes, is a prostitute? If it be true, the subject should be taken up very differently from what it has been; if it be erroneous, it should be corrected, and this foul blot upon the metropolitan female character should be wiped away.' But surely the very statement must be its own ample refutation. It *is not*, it *cannot be* true, nor even an approach to truth.

These differences are so very wide, as to be really marvellous. How far the causes of discrepancy, enumerated by the *Foreign Quarterly Reviewer*, are adequate to account for it in its full extent, I shall not take time to inquire. Any *data* on which an accurate decision could rest, appear to be far from satisfactory.

One thing, however, I must notice, as having forcibly struck me, respecting the smaller estimates of the number of unfortunate females in London – the estimates, I mean, which state it so low as seven, eight or even ten thousand; namely, the inconsistency between these estimates and the representations at the same time given of the *number of houses of ill fame* in the metropolis. According to the returns made by Mr Mayne, these amount to 3,335, and this enumeration 'does not include the city, in which also brothels abound'; and, 'The Rev Mr Hughes of Stafford Chapel, Bloomsbury, states that in a space of about 700 yards in circumference [St Giles Rookery], there are twenty-four houses of ill-fame, in which the average number of occupants is ten' [*Female Virtue. . . . A Discourse* by Revd Dr Edgar of Belfast, p. 9]. Of course, we should be running into a grievous miscalculation, were we to adopt the number of such houses in this particular locality as a ratio of estimate for the whole of London, or even the number of inmates in each of them as the average for all other houses of the same description. Were we to proceed on the latter assumption, the 3,335 brothels would contain 33,350 inmates; and these would be exclusive of the vast number of prostitutes of a more secret description; of whom Mr Tait [*Magdelanism, op. cit.*] makes the number in Edinburgh considerably larger than that of the more common and openly abandoned. This writer . . . makes the 'houses of bad fame, including houses of assignation, licensed taverns, and eating houses where sexual intercourse is tolerated' about 200; the average number of girls who board and lodge in these houses, he estimates at three to each . . . Mr Tait's careful inquiries no doubt satisfied him as to the correctness of this average. It does, however, seem a low one. According to police returns for Glasgow, the average to each of the houses of bad fame (not, however, taking in the variety of descriptions of houses included by Mr Tait) is *seven*. A respected city missionary . . . makes the number of houses larger, and the average complement of each less – *four* instead of *seven*.

Suppose we should take the average for the houses of bad fame in London at *five* instead of *ten*, this will still yield us the aggregate of 16,675; and this, independently of the city, and independently too of all those classes of prostitutes that are not included among the occupants of brothels, respecting whom Mr Mayne says 'That in his opinion, there is no means of ascertaining the number of female servants, milliners, and women in the middle and upper classes of society who might properly be classed with prostitutes.' It must, at one glance, be apparent, that estimate it as you will, the 7,000, or even the highest of Mr Mayne's numbers, the 10,000, for the entire amount of prostitution in London, must be much below the truth.

The careful estimates of Wardlaw and his sources admirably demonstrate the difficulties of estimating the extent of prostitution in the major cities of early Victorian Britain. The war of the statistics, however, made little difference to the activities of the anti-vice crusaders. By 1842 Talbot and his allies felt strong enough to press parliament to change the law in a puritan direction. The London Society for the Protection of Young Females framed a Bill through their solicitor and submitted it to the Home Secretary. The Tory Government was headed by Sir Robert Peel, who had created the Metropolitan Police a decade and a half earlier. Peel, however, had no sympathy with puritan proposals which would increase police powers to threaten the pleasures of male libertines. The government refused to back the Bill.

The London Society refused to accept defeat. They chose to exploit the legislative loophole which allowed members of the House of Lords to introduce Bills into parliament without government consent. The evangelical Bishop of Exeter, a notorious reactionary who had opposed the 1832 Reform Bill, agreed to become the leading light. As a Lord Spiritual, he was in a position to exploit the loophole, and accordingly introduced 'A Bill for the more effectual Suppression of Brothels, and of trading in Seduction and Prostitution' into the Lords on 17 May 1844. The Bill contained several wide-ranging powers, notably that 'if any person shall by any means procure or solicit to knowingly act in the procurement or solicitation of the illicit intercourse of the sexes between other parties, such person so procuring or soliciting . . . shall be guilty of a misdemeanour' and liable to punishment of up to two years in prison with or without hard labour.

The Bill proceeded smoothly through its first and second readings. The debate on the second reading on 14 June, however, showed their Lordships at their worst. A large part of the proceedings rambled through the side issue of whether the Dean and Chapter of Westminster owned twenty-four brothels in a London area known as the Almonry. No objections to the Bill were uttered in the second reading, opponents of the Bill being content to allow Exeter and the puritans to waste their time. The government, however, had no intention of allowing the Bill to become law. At its third reading on 9 July, opposition to the Bill emerged fully armed. Lord Foley stated what became a standard objection to tightening the law on brothels, the Earl of Galloway made an eloquent defence of the Bill on the grounds of the inadequacy of the existing law, but the government wheeled out its biggest gun in the person of the Duke of Wellington, and under assault from the former prime minister, the Bishop of Exeter surrendered.

Debate on the third reading of the Brothels Suppression Bill, 9 July 1844

Lord Foley expressed a fear that any attempt to put such houses down by summary means would only lead to their transfer and re-establishment in other parts of the town, at present free from such nuisances. He thought the law, as it at present stood, sufficient to abate the evil, but whether that were so or not, he feared that even if their Lordships passed the measure, they would find it impossible to carry its provisions into execution. He did not think the subject had undergone sufficient consideration, and he thought any measure on a subject so important should not have been brought forward without full enquiry. He should, therefore, move as an amendment that the Bill be read a third time that day six months.

The Earl of Galloway regretted that unexpected opposition to the Bill had arisen at the eleventh hour, and sincerely hoped the advice of the noble Lord for its defeat would not be heeded. . . . Their Lordships were reminded in the preamble to the Bill, that by the 25th Geo. II, c.36, Parliament had given encouragement for the prosecution of disorderly houses, under which terms were included both gaming houses and brothels; but the machinery enacted had been found too cumbrous, the process too dilatory, so that for the more ready suppression of the first – namely the gaming houses – Parliament had been obliged to give additional powers, and offenders might be prosecuted under the terms of the Metropolitan Police Act, the 2nd and 3rd Victoria, and dealt with by summary conviction before the Magistrate. . . . Now the supporters of this Bill contended that the demoralizing influence of brothels . . . were yet more extensive than those of gaming houses, and that no argument could have been brought for the suppression of the latter by summary process, which might not be made to apply with still greater force to the former . . .

The Duke of Wellington . . . Having informed himself on the subject, he had now to state, that certainly the desire of the Government was very earnest to mitigate any evil resulting from the establishments alluded to; but there was a difficulty of carrying into execution such measures as were proposed in this Bill. It appeared to them that those measures were very stringent, and would require a variety of arrangements to enable the Government and the magistracy to carry this Bill into execution, which measures certainly had not been sufficiently considered in that view, or even as to the propriety of adopting them, supposing that there were means of executing them. Under these circumstances, he recommended his right reverend Friend not to press the measure further on the consideration of the House.

The Bishop of Exeter, after what had fallen from the noble Duke, would be very sorry to press the Bill one moment longer on their Lordships' attention. He rejoiced to trace such expressions of sympathy on this subject from both sides of the House with respect to the object of the Bill, and he hoped that Government, seeing the great importance of the subject, would take it into their consideration with a view to the production of a measure next Session more likely to accomplish the end he had in view.

The Earl of Mountcashell regretted exceedingly that this Bill was about to be abandoned. The evils it was calculated to suppress were of the most alarming character, particularly the horrid trade in seduction, which was carried to an incredible extent in this metropolis. . . . The longer that measure was delayed the more stringent its provisions must be made.

Bill withdrawn.

The puritans were appalled by this débâcle. On 26 July James Talbot rushed out a pamphlet entitled *The Miseries of Prostitution*, in which he outlined the arguments for the Bill, gave the Bill in its entirety, and concluded:

The Miseries of Prostitution

Thus, for the present, the hope of a better law has been prostrated; and the crime of trading in prostitution will, for a little while, continue . . . It is not necessary to scrutinize the motives of those who opposed, or were instrumental in causing the withdrawal of the Bishop of Exeter's Bill. They must be left to their own reflections. They have undoubtedly attained an unenviable notoriety, which will not be easily obliterated. That the 'brothel interest' should find advocates amongst those who profit by it, is not wonderful, but that, in the face of the whole country (whatever might have been the private feeling), any one claiming for himself nobility of rank and dignity of character, should stand up and attempt to put aside a measure with such strong claims to justice and humanity, as well as tending to promote the moral welfare of the country, is truly astonishing.

What is more astonishing is the fact that Talbot and his allies were surprised by the failure of the Bill. Their belief that the brothel interest lay behind the defeat, and that the Duke of Wellington could be fingered in this manner, is a powerful indication of the fantasy world in which the puritans lived. It is equally remarkable that Talbot could believe that his sect spoke for the whole country. The themes set down here – corruption of the legislature by the brothel interest, the defeat of the popular will by illegitimate means, and the hypocrisy of the nobility, were none the less to recur time and time again in the propaganda of the anti-vice crusade over the next forty years.

3. Legislation and Investigation: the 1849 Act and the Perambulations of William Logan

Following the débâcle of the 1844 Act, the puritans had to accept that they could not secure any legislation against brothels in the climate of the time. They therefore switched their attention to the seduction of women by trickery for immoral purposes. This was a cause which even libertines could not object to. Accordingly, in 1848 the evangelical Bishop of Oxford, backed by Lord Brougham and other evangelicals, brought in a Bill for the Protection of Females. Their initial efforts failed, but formed the basis of a successful Act against seduction forced through in 1849. The debate on the Bill illustrates clearly the state of play concerning morality and prostitution in the middle years of the nineteenth century.

Debate on the Bill for the Protection of Females, second reading,
5 June 1848

The Bishop of OXFORD rose to move the Second Reading . . . In proceeding with this measure, it would, on the present occasion at least, not be necesary for him to trouble their Lordships at any length . . . By the Bill which he held in his hand no attempt was made for the suppression of brothels; but it was, on the contrary, intended for the prevention of one great evil to which this metropolis and other large cities were exposed; he alluded to the practices of entrapping, by unfair arts, young and unsuspecting females. From the best returns which he could obtain, it did appear that within the metropolis there were as many as 80,000 women who lived by prostitution; and there was every reason to believe that at least one fourth of that number were brought to the deplorable state . . . by the arts against which this Bill was directed. It was a fact . . . that many persons made an infamous livelihood by waiting at the different accesses from the country to this great city for the purpose of entrapping unwary young persons . . . inducing those without friends or a knowledge of London to accompany them to their abodes of infamy where, in a condition often of unconsciousness, their ruin was effected . . .

He knew as well as anybody that they could not by Act of Parliament make either men or women moral; but there was a principle of the law which recognised the duty of protecting those who needed protection from the arts of those who sought to make a profit of their unwariness and simplicity . . .

Debate on the Bill's third reading,

11 July 1848

Lord Denham said that . . . he thought it would, if passed, not only be ineffectual for its purposes, but fraught with greater evils than it was intended to remedy. In the first place it would lead to attempts to extort money by accusations of the commission of the offence; and, in the next place, he felt pretty sure that an attempt to enforce the measure of that kind would fail in a court of justice, after very offensive and scandalous exposures . . . Under the law as it stood, there was no difficulty in inflicting punishment when it had once been proved that a party had been decoyed into a house of ill fame; the difficulty was to procure the necessary evidence. The injured party came before the court, already polluted, to give an account of the manner in which she had been led astray, and was not likely to be very scrupulous in her statements . . . It was the difficulty inherent in the case which made legislation on such a question almost impossible . . .

Their Lordships rejected the Bill by 28 votes to 21, apparently convinced by Lord Denham's arguments that legislation was almost impossible and mindful of the risk of extortion. However, they underestimated the determination of the puritans, who immediately came back with an almost identical Bill – a step which was highly dubious under the rules of procedure but made their intentions to get the Bill through very clear.

Debate on the Protection of Women Bill,

13 July 1848

Lord Brougham said it would be in the recollection of the House that the Protection of Females Bill was rejected a few evenings ago: but as he thought that it was most desirable to obtain the chief object of that measure, he had prepared another Bill on the subject . . . which would impose penalties only in case of the seduction of virtuous and correct females by fraud and covin . . .

Lord Campbell . . . certainly was unwilling to throw any impediment in the way of his noble friend. What he wished to state was that when a Bill for the attainment of a particular object had been rejected during the course of a Session, he doubted whether, consistent with the Orders of the House, a Bill for the same purpose could be brought forward during the same Session . . .

Lord Brougham said he would propose . . . to take the Second Reading on Tuesday; and if upon conferring with his noble friends opposite . . . he found the feeling was against him, he would not proceed further this Session.

Lord Denham said . . . he felt the greatest apprehension and alarm at any such measure as that now proposed.. The subject was, however, one on which every one must feel great anxiety; for his own part he could only observe, that it was only after much consideration that he had come to the conclusion that such measures would do more harm than good.

Lord Denham clearly realised that although what was being proposed was open to objection, the Bill now had too strong a head of steam behind it to be stopped. In moving the second reading on 25 May 1849, the Bishop of Oxford stated that the Lord Chief Justice of the Queen's Bench had written to him to say he would not oppose the Bill, noting that this 'was a peculiar satisfaction to him; for last year his noble and learned Friend had conceeved it to be his duty to oppose the Bill . . .'. Lord Campbell criticised the Bill as producing a worse situation than the Common Law it was intended to strengthen, but, like the Lord Chief Justice, was not prepared to oppose the second reading. There is a strong sense that the government was prepared to allow the moral purity lobby a victory; perhaps because, as the MP Anstey said in the second reading in the Commons, 'there was out of doors a great deal of morbid and unnatural excitement on the subject of the measure'. The Bill duly passed all stages in both Houses of Parliament. The critical comments of three MPs who noted their dissent in the third reading in the Commons are set out below as representing a viewpoint which normally triumphed when puritan legislation was proposed.

Debate on the third reading of the Protection of Women Bill,

25 July 1849

Mr HUME said that he could not allow this extraordinary measure to pass without saying a few words by way of protesting against it . . . he protested against this kind of interference altogether. There was a certain class of persons who were never at rest unless they were showing intolerance to their neighbours, or making loud professions of superior sanctity. That was a class whom he always looked upon with suspicion, because in his dealings with them he had always found them the readiest to impose upon others, and the least ready to do justice.

Mr ROEBUCK also begged to enter his protest against this ill-considered and crude piece of legislation, which he described as the result of a species of cant which was almost as dangerous as vice.

Mr MOWATT had also felt himself obliged to oppose the Bill, because it was calculated to mislead the people for whose benefit they affected to legislate, namely, the parents of females in humble life, by teaching them to dispense with the moral education and training of their children, and lean only upon the legislature.

These protests were to no avail. The Bill passed into law on 28 July 1849 and read as follows: *An Act to protect Women from Fraudulent Practices for Procuring their Defilement 128 13 Vict. cap. LXXVI.*

I. For the better preventing the heinous Offence of procuring the defiling of Women, which certain infamous Persons do most wickedly practice, Be it enacted by the Queen's Excellent Majesty . . . That if any Person shall, by false Pretences, false Representations, or other fraudulent means, procure any woman or child under the Age of Twenty-one Years to have illicit carnal Connexion with any Man, such Person shall be guilty of a Misdemeanour, and shall, being duly convicted thereof, suffer Imprisonment for a term not exceeding Two Years, with hard Labour.

II. And be it enacted, That where any Prosecutor or other Person shall appear before any Court on recognizance to prosecute or give evidence against any Person charged with any Offence against this Act, every such Court is hereby authorised and empowered, whether any Bill of Indictment for such charge be actually preferred, to order Payment of the Costs and Expenses of the Prosecutor and Witnesses for the Prosecution, in the same manner as Courts are now by Law authorised and empowered to order the same in Cases of Prosecutions for Felony.

III. And be it enacted, That every Order for the Payment of any money by virtue of this Act shall be made out and delivered by the proper Officer of the Court unto such Prosecutor or other Person upon the same Terms and in the same Manner in all respects as Orders for the Payment of Costs are now made in Cases of Felony, and the Treasurer or other Person when any such Order shall be made shall be and he is hereby required, upon Sight of such Order, forthwith to pay to the Person therein named, or to any one duly authorised in that Behalf, the Money in such Order mentioned, and such Treasurer or other

Person shall be allowed the same in passing his Accounts.

This was indeed an 'ill considered and crude' piece of legislation, which has little of substance about it and which does not even read well. What effect it had it is difficult to see. Certainly when the genesis of the 1885 Criminal Law Amendment Act is considered, the inadequacy of the law to protect women under 21 from procuration was considered a serious matter, while the 1849 Act seems to have been regarded as a dead letter.

It is clear that the Act represented a hollow triumph for the moral purity lobby. They remained a marginal force with little political muscle. The most that can be said for them is that they remained active investigators and interventionists in the dark world of commercial sex, and at their best produced limited but useful evidence of the underworld of prostitution. The anti-vice crusade had become a well-organised and deeply entrenched phenomenon with outposts in most major cities. A distinctive cadre of missionaries engaged in the reclamation of prostitutes became a feature of Victorian Britain. The most eminent of those driven by religious conviction to seek fallen women in the streets and rescue them for virtue was of course William Gladstone. However, Gladstone was only the most prominent member of a reclamation crusade of considerable extent.

A more typical member of this dedicated band was William Logan. He began his work in 1838, and by 1843 had amassed enough experience to contribute to the controversies of that period a pamphlet entitled *An Exposure . . . of Female Prostitution,* (Glasgow), 1843). His most interesting work is, however, *The Great Social Evil,* published in 1871, and from which the following extracts are taken. This was a record of three decades of rescue work remarkable both for the wide scope of his investigations, and the extent to which in each town he could find active and flourishing anti-vice organisations. In mid-Victorian Britain, anti-vice work was clearly a major activity for the religiously inclined. Logan's fascination with the life of fallen women – part horrified recoil, part sociological investigation, part hunt for souls – is uniquely Victorian.

The Great Social Evil, *William Logan, 1871,*

Personal Notes

St Giles, London, pp. 30–2

Early in January 1838, I commenced labouring as a city missionary, under the superintendence of David Nasmith, the esteemed Founder of Town and City

Missions, and was appointed to visit in the immediate neighbourhood of Drury Lane, London. The principal thoroughfare in the district has been designated by a distinguished novelist as 'Gibbett Street', which was the great rendezvous for London pick-pockets, harlots and beggars. In one house I found from eight to ten miserable young women. The mistress of this vile den was one of the most forbidding creatures a person could look on – a sort of demon in human form, such as has been described to the life by Sir Walter Scott. One of the girls, about sixteen years of age, of fascinating appearance 'like a stricken deer', occupied a seat by herself. It was evident she was nearing her journey's end. A few kind earnest words were addressed to her about the importance of coming without delay to Christ for pardon. More than thirty years have passed since that interview, but I have a vivid recollection of the somewhat hopeful, yet dejected look of that pale, comely countenance, as it seemed to say, 'Is it possible that there is mercy for a poor wanderer such as I?' . . . This case was the first which specially attracted my attention to the subject of prostitution.

Proceeding one forenoon to visit a tenement in the same street I entered a dark passage, and ascended a few steps to what might be called the second landing . . . there was no stair to be found. I groped about in the dark, but as far as the right arm could reach, I felt nothing. There seemed to be a plank stretching across the chasm at my feet, and on this I ventured, but after advancing a little, being unable to feel anything like a wall, I thought it most prudent to retrace my steps. I did so as cautiously as possible, and was about to descend when I heard the sound of human voices . . . I therefore got down on my hands and knees and moved along very slowly and cautiously till I reached the other end of the plank . . . I fancied that the people above me heard my movements, for the sound of voices as of persons talking in a kind of whisper reached me. Arrived at the top of the stair I knocked at the door, which was opened, and I observed at a glance that the house was a third class brothel in which I found several young men and women. One of the young men said, with a self-condemned look, 'I am not, sir, where I ought to be, and shall be glad to accept of one of your tracts.' After a short and somewhat hopeful interview, I retraced my steps, getting along the narrow plank in the same way as before, and on reaching the first stair felt inexpressibly grateful to recognise a few rays of heaven's light, which enabled me to descend in safety . . .

Leeds

In a few months Mr Nasmith requested me to go to Leeds, as a Town mission had been established there, and an agent was wanted. There I met with a cordial reception from the Rev. John Ely, the Rev. Dr R. Winter Hamilton,

Mr John Wade and others who felt deeply interested in the social and religious welfare of the inhabitants . . . During 1839 I succeeded in reclaiming, for a time at least, some twelve girls, assisted with the missionary brethren in rescuing another ten, and with the generous and valuable assistance of Mr Edward Baines MP (father of the present MP for Leeds) was instrumental in closing several well known improper houses . . .

In common with others I had often read and heard a great many general statements as to the alleged number of fallen women . . . I resolved to do what I could to obtain as accurate information as possible on the subject, and, accordingly, commenced and visited, in the course of the forenoon, almost every house of ill-fame in Leeds. The following is a summary of what appeared in the *Leeds Mercury*, in January 1840, but the calculations refer only to the *third* class houses.

Number of houses of ill-fame, as near as could be ascertained	175
Number of harlots (an average of four in each house)	700
Number of 'bullies' or 'fancy men' about	350
Number of mistresses of such houses	175
Total living directly on prostitutes	1,225
Number of visits of men to each house weekly	80
The girls receive on an average 30 shillings weekly	£1,050
Robberies – 2 shillings six pence from each visitor is a low average	£1,750
Spent on drink, 2 shillings by each visitor	£1,400
Total for prostitutes weekly	£4,200

Glasgow

Towards the close of 1841 I was appointed by the Directors of the Glasgow City Mission to visit one of the most depraved parts of the city, in which I found first, second, and third class brothels. Stirling Street, which had long been notorious for improper houses, formed part of the district. At No. 8, not fewer than three flats, each containing six or seven apartments, were occupied by this disreputable class. 'No. 8' was known even in London by the supporters of such dens, as the 'Three Decker'. I occasionally left tracts at the doors of those three houses, but felt it imprudent to enter alone. In the same street I met with a number of poor but respectable people, who felt much annoyed, especially at night and on Sundays, with the inmates and visitors of those houses. The Police Act respecting brothels was not so stringent at that time as it is now, but I resolved to try and rid the street of those pest houses, not only for the sake of the decent neighbours, but because it was a general thoroughfare on Sabbath for persons attending places of worship. By the valuable assistance of the Rev. Dr Heugh, Sir James Anderson . . . William Campbell, of Tillichewan, backed by Henry Miller, then Chief Superintendent of Police, and one or two Glasgow papers, Stirling Street was in two or three years cleared of its brothels – three second class and one first – and the same houses are now occupied by respectable tradesmen.

Bradford
On the 1st March 1850, the Bradford Town Mission was started, and I was appointed its general agent or superintendent. . . . The Chief Constable for Bradford stated, in his report of October 1st 1851, that the number of known brothels within the borough was 42; the number of known prostitutes residing in them was 109; the number of prostitutes residing in 13 beerhouses in the borough 21 – total 130. I believe the number of houses of ill fame in Bradford, at that time, to be pretty correct; but from my own knowledge of the lower parts of the town, I have no hesitation in stating that the number of girls referred to as occupying these houses to be considerably under the mark.

Cork
In February 1848, I visited Ireland, and spent several weeks in the city of Cork. Richard Dowdon, the late Mayor, kindly gave me a note of introduction to the officials of all the principal public institutions in the city . . . Alderman Roche introduced me to a philanthropic gentleman, who furnished me with a valuable paper on the subject of prostitution. . . . He thus writes . . . 'It appears by the census returns, taken by the constabulary in 1841, that the city of Cork contained within the borough bounds, a population, in round numbers, of 80,000 . . . There were 85 regular brothels in the city, in which there were 356 public prostitutes . . . there are at least 100 which are termed 'privateers' who have not yet turned out to the streets, but are living in private lodgings. The class of persons from whom prostitutes are supplied, are generally low dressmakers and servants; manure collectors, who are sent very young to the streets for the purpose, have also furnished their quota; poverty, vicious habits, idleness, ambition for dress, together with the seductive arts of what are termed 'procuresses', are the great causes of prostitution.

There is scarcely an instance in which virtuous females first resorted to the

streets, but were almost invariably previously seduced; they then afterwards, for
some time, continue what is termed 'privateers', but eventually become
degraded and turn to the streets. Prostitutes are not received into the superior
brothels, except upon a sort of recommendation from another of the same
class. If it is known that any of them had been on the streets, they are never
afterwards received into these houses. They pay their mistress about 8 shillings
a week for their board; their surplus earnings are appropriated to their own
use. Some of them are known to have saved money, and the keeper of one
brothel is at this moment supposed to be possessed of a sum exceeding £500.
The age of prostitutes in this city varies from sixteen to thirty years . . . Few,
however, if any of them, reach the prescribed term of human existence. Violent
deaths, diseases, and constitutions prematurely worn out generally consign
them to an early grave . . .

An Act of Parliament is . . . the only hope left; and in order to legislate with
any probability of success, the origin of the evil must be traced out, and when
discovered, a very stringent clause should be introduced to bear upon it. Now,
it cannot be denied that man is the great source from whence the misery
consequent upon prostitution flows . . . therefore the law should be directly
levelled against him, and whenever convicted of seducing a female, a portion of
his property (if any, otherwise imprisonment), should be appropriated to her
maintenance, if found deserving of it, or given as a donation to an Asylum. A
clause should also be introduced authorising the transportation of any person
convicted of procuring virtuous females for the purposes of prostitution.

Whilst engaged as a city missionary in Glasgow I visited for some time the
Magdalene Institution, and for several years the Central police office, and
the Lock Hospital weekly, which enabled me to form a more correct idea of the
system. I wish it to be distinctly understood that the rules which regulate
the nefarious system in London are substantially the same in Leeds,
Manchester, Edinburgh, Glasgow, Dublin, Cork etc.

Part Two: Uneasy Toleration, 1844–1864

4. *The Debate on the Great Social Evil*

Despite the puritan attack and the unease of the 'respectable', the rights of prostitutes to ply their trade – and their customers to purchase their wares – remained unchallenged in the mid-nineteenth century. The following extracts demonstrate the complexity of mid-Victorian attitudes to prostitution, tolerating it without acceptance. The strength of *laissez-faire*, and the reluctance of magistrates to challenge it, is illustrated by the first item, a newspaper report concerning a meeting of the Aldermen of the City of London.

The Times, *21 February 1844*

Alderman WILSON presented a petition from the inhabitants of the ward of Castlechurchyard, complaining that the neighbourhood of St Paul's churchyard was greatly disturbed and disgusted by the behaviour of women of the town at night, and praying that the Court would take some means of abating so serious a nuisance. He had, upon the representation of the circumstances to him, advised the petitioners to apply to the Commissioner of the City Police, who, however, informed him that the Magistrates would not assist his efforts to remove the women of the town from the place described as being subject to the nuisance. The Alderman moved, that the petition be referred to the Police Committee.

Mr Keating (of St Paul's churchyard), one of the petitioners, said in answer to questions put by members of the Court, that he and others of the petitioners waited upon the Commissioner of the City Police, according to the recommendation of Alderman Wilson, and were informed by Mr Harvey that there was no use in taking up the women of the town, for the magistrates dismissed them without inflicting any punishment.

Alderman COPELAND: A more gratuitous piece of impertinence I never heard of than that upon the part of the Commissioner.

Alderman FAIRBROTHER said it was most ridiculous for the Commissioner to make such a statement. If the Commissioner or his men could not establish a case against the unfortunate women whom they might think proper to take into custody, why should the magistrates not dismiss them? (Hear, hear.) These poor creatures must be somewhere; in Regent Street they were infinitely more numerous than they were in St Paul's churchyard; and why, if acts of disorder were not proved against them, should they be punished with imprisonment, or with the bad treatment which they often suffered without being brought before magistrates at all! He for one would not imprison a wretched woman merely because she was brought before him by a policeman, and he cared nothing for the opinion of the Commissioner on the question. . . .

Alderman BROWN said the petitioners complained of what they considered to be a great nuisance, and upon stating the nature of it to the Commissioner, and asking for his interpretation, what did he say? That there was no use in it, for the magistrates dismissed the accused . . . The Commissioner ought to have said, 'Gentlemen, we cannot commit women of the town for walking the streets. The streets are open to them as they are to us; but I must do the magistrates the justice to say that when any act of disorder is committed by these women, they uniformly carry the law into effect.' (Hear, hear.)

Alderman WOOD said the police not only brought women of the town but reputed thieves before the magistrates, but evidence was necessary introductory to punishment. Indeed, it was frequently the case that the magistrates were obliged to reprove the police for apprehending persons without having the slightest ground for taking them into custody . . .

Toleration was, however, a cold and limited virtue, as illustrated by the next two extracts, both from Henry Mayhew's series of interviews with London's street people. Henry Mayhew was one of the few Victorian observers to give the poor a sympathetic hearing.

'A Flower Girl'

Some of these girls are, as I have stated, of an immoral character, and some of them are sent out by their parents to make out a livelihood by prostitution. One of this class, whom I saw, had come out of prison a short time previously. She was not nineteen, and had been sentenced about a twelvemonth before to three months imprisonment with hard labour 'for heaving her shoe', as she said, 'at the Lord Mayor, to get a comfortable lodging, for she was tired of being about the streets'. After this she was locked up for breaking the lamps in the street. She alleged that her motive for this was a belief that by committing some such act she might be able to get into an asylum for females. She was sent out into the streets by her father and mother, at the age of nine, to sell flowers.

Her father used to supply her with the money to buy the flowers, and she used to take the proceeds of the day's work home to her parents. She used to be out frequently till past midnight, and seldom or never got home before nine. She associated only with flower girls of loose character. The result may be imagined.

She could not state positively that her parents were aware of the manner in which she got the money she took home to them. She supposes that they must have imagined what her practices were. He used to give her no supper if she 'didn't bring home a good bit of money'. Her father and mother did little or no work all this while. They lived on what she brought home. At thirteen years old she was sent to prison (she stated) 'for selling combs in the street' (but it was winter, and there were no combs to be had). She was incarcerated fourteen days, and when liberated she returned to her former practices. The very night that she came home from gaol her father sent her out into the streets again. She continued in this state, her father and mother living upon her, until about twelve months before I received this account from her, when her father turned her out of his house because she didn't bring home money enough.

She then went into Kent, hop picking, and there fell in with a beggar, who accosted her while she was sitting under a tree. He said, 'You have got a very bad pair of shoes on; come with me, and you shall have some better ones.' She consented, and walked with him into the village close by, where they stood out in the middle of the streets, and the man began addressing the people. 'My good kind Christians, me and my poor wife is ashamed to appear before you in the state we are in.' She remained with this person all the winter . . . In the spring she returned to the flower selling, but scarcely got any money either by that or other means. At last she grew desperate, and wanted to go back to prison. She broke the lamps outside the Mansion House, and was sentenced to fourteen days imprisonment. She had been out of prison nearly three weeks when I saw her, and was in training to go into an asylum. She was sick and tired, she said, of her life.

'The Sixteen-Year-Old Street-walker'

A good looking girl of sixteen gave me the following awful statement. Her hands were swollen with cold.

'I am an orphan. When I was ten I was sent to service as maid-of-all-work, in a small tradesman's family. It was a hard place, and my mistress used me very cruelly, beating me often. I stood my mistress's ill-treatment for about six months . . . at last I ran away. I got to Mrs —'s, a low lodging house. I didn't know before there was such a place. I heard of it from some girls at the Glasshouse [baths and washhouses], where I went for shelter. I went with them to have a half-pennyworth of coffee, and they took me to the lodging house. I then had three shillings, and stayed there about three months, and did nothing wrong, living on the three shillings and what I pawned my clothes for, as I got some pretty good things away with me. In the lodging house, I saw nothing but what was bad, and heard nothing what was bad. I was laughed at, and told to swear. They said, "Look at her for a d— modest fool" – sometimes worse than that, until by degrees I got to be as bad as they were.

'During this time I used to see boys and girls from ten and twelve years old sleeping together, but understood nothing wrong. I had never heard of such places before I ran away. I can neither read nor write. My mother was a good woman, and I wish I'd had her to run away to. I saw things between almost children that I can't describe to you – very often I saw them, and that shocked me.

'At the month's end, when I was beat out, I met with a young man of fifteen – I myself was going on for twelve years old – and he persuaded me to take up with him. I stayed with him three months in the same lodging house, living with him as his wife, though we were mere children, and being true to him. At the three months' end he was taken up for picking pockets, and got six months. I was sorry, for he was kind to me; though I was made ill through him; so I broke some windows in St Paul's Churchyard to get into prison to get cured. I had a month in the Compter [prison], and came out well. I was scolded very much in the Compter, on account of the state I was in, being so young. I had 2s 6d given to me when I came out, and was forced to go into the streets for a living.

'I continued walking the streets for three years, sometimes making a good deal of money, sometimes none, feasting one day and starving the next. The bigger girls could persuade me to do anything they liked with my money. I was never happy all the time, but I could get no character and could not get out of the life. I lodged all this time at a lodging house in Kent Street. They were all thieves and bad girls. I have known between three and four dozen boys and girls sleep in one room. The beds were horrid filthy and full of vermin.

'There was very wicked carryings on. The boys, if any difference, was the worst. We lay packed on a full night, a dozen boys and girls squeezed into one bed. That was very often the case – some at the foot and some at the top – boys and girls all mixed. I can't go into all the particulars, but whatever could take place in words and acts between boys and girls did take place, and in the midst of the others . . . Some boys and girls slept without any clothes, and would dance about the room that way. I have seen them, and, wicked as I was, I felt ashamed . . .

'At three years' end I stole a piece of beef from a butcher. I did it to get into prison. I was sick of the life I was leading, and didn't know how to get out of it. I had a month for stealing. When I got out I passed two days and a night in the streets doing nothing wrong, and then went and threatened to break Messrs —s' windows again. I did that to get into prison again, for when I lay quiet of a night in prison I thought things over, and considered what a shocking life I was leading, and how my health might be ruined completely, and I thought I would stick to prison rather than go back to such a life. I got six months for threatening. When I got out I broke a lamp next morning for the same purpose, and had a fortnight. That was the last time I was in prison. I have since been leading the same life as I told you of for three years, and lodging at the same houses, and seeing the same goings on. I hate such a life now more than ever. I am willing to do any work that I can in washing and cleaning . . .'

White slavery became the central plank of the puritan campaign of the 1880s, but the following case, taken from a newspaper report in 1854, shows that the techniques of the white slaver were well developed thirty years earlier. This case, however, dealt with French and Belgian girls trapped in an English brothel for the use of English men, and did not arouse the heated feelings that the export of English women to the Continent did in the later campaign.

The Times, *22 June 1854*

A case was held on Tuesday before Chief Justice Jervis, which must have excited the greatest disgust in every man of ordinary feeling . . . Surely the mind of a man, however profligate, must revolt at the idea of entering a mere warehouse of brutal passion, in which women are bought and sold like cattle in Smithfield market. The thing has attained the dimensions of a regular trade. Some villain – generally a foreigner – chooses a proper situation for an establishment of this kind; he has his agents and his correspondents abroad; he directs them to look out, generally in France or Belgium, for such young women as are best adapted to his purpose, and that purpose is nothing less than to make his profit out of their prostitution.

Such a person was the defendant in the case tried the day before yesterday in the Court of Common Pleas. His name is MARMAYSEE, and he carries on his infamous business in Newman Street and Oxford Street. The girls imported by him are, from the moment they are consigned to him, completely within his power. In a strange country, ignorant of the language and customs of the place, unable to find their way from one street to another, they are entirely at his mercy. His method of dealing with them appears to be this; In the first place, they are bound to pay him so much a week for board and lodging. Then, they must give up one half of all the money they receive from the visitors of the house. Then, any article of clothing which they may desire, or of which they stand in absolute need – any purchase they may wish to make, must pass absolutely through his hands. All these items of expenditure are defrayed from the moiety of the receipts which the unfortunate girls ostensibly are allowed to consider to call their own. It is scarcely necessary to say that, with so many opportunities for running up a bill against the inmates, MARMAYSEE had but seldom occasion to hand over a balance of any kind . . .

If such things exist among us, it is right that we should know they are there . . . As no system of police can be introduced into private society, and as public opinion must take the place of it, it is but right that public opinion should be well informed. Such establishments as those of the wretched MARMAYSEE exist in London, and the proprietors find them a gainful and profitable concern. It is not for us to point out any direct way of meeting the evil. As matters stand at present, any rascal who keeps a brothel is liable to indictment and perhaps, there is not sufficient activity displayed in the employment of this remedy. Such as it is, however, it must necessarily be imperfect, and fail to meet the evil. There must be something thoroughly wrong in the state of public feeling when establishments for the gratification of the sheerest bestiality – if the English language contained a more forcible expression we would employ it – can flourish and afford a profitable investment of capital; but they have their proprietors, their foreign correspondents, and are as regularly conducted as any other business establishment in the three kingdoms . . .

'The Delicate Question': In response to puritan calls for action against street-walkers, a prostitute wrote to *The Times* early in January 1858, lifting the veil on a situation which the respectable *Times* took very seriously. The letter was carried on 4 January 1858.

Sir: Certain persons have, as you know, commenced a crusade against London prostitutes, and, if one of that abandoned sisterhood may presume to address you, grant me your attention.

The precept and example set me by parents, now, thank God, in their graves; the education likewise 'thrown away' upon me, and my subsequent experience as a governess in a highly respectable family, were not necessary to the conviction that the class among which I may be numbered consists of outcasts whose undisguised pursuit is an offence to the laws of God and man.

I know that we are cut off from the moral, social and religious worlds. . . . We need not be told of our ruin and degradation, because we never 'fall' without being alive to the fact. A woman seduced may forgive her wrongs . . . it is impossible for her to forget what she is; society will not permit her to do so . . . Do not suppose, then, that I would attempt to defend what transpires nightly in the Haymarket, in Coventry Street, or wherever women of my caste congregate. I do not ask you to countenance anything of the kind. No, Sir, give 'Vice its own image' and do your duty.

But, while you yourself refrain from going a step too far, pray give a warning to others. It is one thing to put down a nuisance. It is another to persecute individuals. I will anticipate much that may fairly be said, and admit that if I live avowedly in defiance of those regulations which the community has established as essential to its well being . . . I must expect to be checked in such openly vicious courses, for I believe the liberty of the subject should end where injustice to others begins. But pray tell those good gentlemen who are bent on 'putting us down', that theirs is not only a delicate, but a difficult undertaking, and they should be careful lest they have more to answer for than they dream of in their philosophy.

The vice of London, Sir, is seen to float upon its surface; let it pass as the weed on its way to the ocean. If it accumulates so as to become offensive, disperse it. If it is otherwise annoying and cannot conveniently be avoided, deal with it accordingly.

Appoint commissioners who are fitted for the office, intelligent, respectable, and responsible gentlemen, and make it worth their while to devote themselves entirely to the reduction of the scandal complained of. Empower these officials to have us taken up and punished for riot or impropriety of any kind. But let not the 'pelting petty officer', the ignorant constable of a few shillings a week, and it may be an unfeeling and unthinking brute, interfere with us as he will. Recollect it was man who made us what we are. It is man who pays for the finery, the rouge and the gin . . . it is man who, when we apply ourselves to industry and honesty, employs us upon starvation wages; and if man had his way, and women's nature were not superior to his, there would be no virtue extant. Say, then, is it for man to persecute even the most profligate among us?

Pray, Sir, think of this, and tell those gentlemen whose speeches I read to act upon it. They may be husbands and fathers . . . and I allow for their parental

Black Sarah of the Ratcliffe Highway. (*The Town*, 8 July 1837. Mary
Evans Picture Library)

solicitude. But if they be Christians they will imitate one who said, 'Go, and sin no more', and not 'move on', 'anywhere, anywhere, out of the world'.

Your humble servant,

One More Unfortunate

The Times, *8 January 1858: Prostitution in London*

In no capital city of Europe is there daily and nightly such a shameless display of prostitution as in London. At Paris, at Vienna, at Berlin, as every one knows, there is plenty of vice; but at least, it is not allowed to parade the streets . . . if anyone would see the evil of which we speak in its full development, let him pass along the Haymarket and its neighbourhood at night, when the night houses and the oyster shops are open. It is not an easy matter to make your way along without molestation. In Regent Street, in the Strand, in Fleet Street, the same nuisance, but in a less degree, prevails. Now, we are well aware, that if all the unfortunate creatures who parade these localities were swept away to-morrow – if the night houses and the oyster shops were closed by the police, we should not have really suppressed immorality. We should, however, have removed the evil from the sight of those who are disgusted and annoyed by its display; and, still more, we should have removed it from the sight of those who probably, had they not been tempted by the sight of those opportunities, would not have fallen into vicious ways at all. . . .

Now, as one practical measure for the discouragement of prostitution, all those night houses and others might be placed under the surveillance of the police. Licences for opening them . . . might be given only in the cases of persons who offered some guarantees of respectability. They might be compelled to close at certain hours; in point of fact the community could tolerate well nigh any degree of inconvenience inflicted upon their frequenters. In two other analogous cases similar evils have been dealt with in this way, and with the happiest results – we speak of gaming houses and betting offices. It is quite certain that persons who are firmly resolved to play and to bet will effect their purpose even now, but at least the sum of the evils resulting from those two vices have been greatly diminished since the community has resolved to withdraw from them its recognition. England should not grant her exquatur to Prostitution.

This is one thing which might be tried. Another would be to give increased force to clauses which, as we believe, already exist in the Police Acts, by which the police are empowered to stop the solicitation and gathering together of prostitutes in the public streets. In such a case we must trample down definitions and exceptional cases with an elephant's foot, and go straight for results.

The puritans continued to pressurise ministers to suppress prostitution – the Great Social Evil, and ministers politely continued to refuse to act. The discussions did little but publicise the problems – a fact which was noted by various newspapers, including *The Times* and the *Lancet*.

The Times, *15 January 1858*

An adjourned meeting was held yesterday at the Chambers of the Society for the Suppression of Vice on this important subject, at which there were present many of the clergy and vestrymen of the parishes of St James, Westminster, St Martin-in-the-Fields, and St Marylebone, and the following resolutions were passed unanimously:

1. That a deputation do wait as early as possible upon Sir George Gray, for the purpose of most respectfully but earnestly representing to Her Majesty's Government the necessity of effectual measures being taken to put down the open exhibition of street prostitution, which in various parts of the metropolis, particularly in the important thoroughfares of the Haymarket, Coventry Street, Regent Street, Portland Place, and other adjacent localities, is carried on with a disregard of public decency and to an extent tolerated in no other capital or city of the civilised world.

2. That such a deputation be instructed to urge upon Her Majesty's Government the following measures, whereby it is believed that the evil complained of may be effectually controlled:
Firstly, the enforcement upon a systematic plan and by means of a department of the police specially appointed and instructed for that purpose, of the provisions of the 2nd and 3rd Victoria, chap 47, in reference to street prostitution, which provisions have in certain localities been heretofore carried out with the best effect, and in others have been ineffectual only because acted upon partially, and not upon any uniform system;
And secondly, for passing an Act for licensing and placing under proper regulations as to supervision and hours of closing all houses of entertainment or for the supply of refreshments intended to be opened to the public after a certain fixed hour, it being a matter of public notoriety that the houses of this description, popularly known as night houses, have, by becoming places of

resort of crowds of prostitutes and other idle and disorderly persons at all hours
of the night, greatly contributed to the present disgraceful exhibition of street
prostitution.

3. That this meeting, understanding that a meeting of delegates from the
metropolitan vestries is to be held to-morrow in the Vestry room of St James's,
Westminster, desires to express its cordial sympathy with the objects of that
meeting – namely, due control of the night houses and the removal of the
public scandal connected with prostitution in the metropolis, and to tender any
support or co-operation which it may be in its power to give for the furtherance
of that object; and that this resolution be communicated to the chairman of
that meeting before 12 o'clock to-morrow.

4. That the attention of the Government be also directed to the great
number of foreign prostitutes systematically imported into this country, and to
the means of controlling this increasing evil.

The Lancet, *24 January 1858*

On Saturday last, a deputation of the vestrymen of St James's, Westminster . . .
called the attention of Sir George Grey, at the Home Office, to the increase of
houses of ill fame in London. They represented that every legal means had
been tried for their suppression, but the law afforded no redress; houses against
which judgement had been obtained being now re-opened. In some cases,
houses in the best streets were so occupied; and sometimes with shops on the
ground floor, where respectable women dealt. They pointed out that the only
law which provided any remedy had not been altered since the time of George
II, and actually required that a morally criminal act should be committed
before a prosecution could be instituted. Of course no information was elicited,
but if the representations of the deputation serve to awaken public attention to
the shameless depravity which disgraces our London streets, it will have
rendered service to the cause of public morals and of public health. The time is
surely past for that blundering hypocrisy which, tightly shutting its eyes in the
presence of vice, ignores its existence because it is not visible. If nothing is to be
done to remedy this evil – the greatest sin of the greatest city – it would be well
that we no longer boast of the morality of a country where the finest streets of
the capital are voluntarily resigned to the dominion of Vice, 'with unchaste
looks, loose gesture, and foul talk', and 'where Virtue has no tongue to check
her pride'.

The letter from 'One More Unfortunate' to *The Times* provoked a lively correspondence, including another letter from a prostitute. This letter, published by *The Times* under the heading 'The Great Social Evil', was the most remarkable of the series.

The Times, *24 February 1858*

Sir, Another 'Unfortunate', but of a class entirely different from the one who has already instructed the public in your columns, presumes to address you. I am a stranger to all the fine sentiments which still linger in the bosom of your correspondent. I have none of those youthful recollections which, contrasting her early days with her present life, aggravate the misery of the latter.

My parents did not give me any education; they did not instil into my mind virtuous precepts nor set me a good example. All my experiences in early life were gleaned among associates who knew nothing of the laws of God but by dim tradition and faint report, and whose chiefest triumphs of wisdom consisted of picking their way through the paths of destitution in which they were cast by cunning evasion or in open defiance of the laws of man . . .

Let me tell you something of my parents. My father's most profitable occupation was bricklaying. When not employed at this, he did anything he could get to do. My mother worked with him in the brickfield, and so did I and a progeny of brothers and sisters; for somehow or other, although my parents occupied a very unimportant space in the world, it pleased God to make them fruitful. We all slept in the same room. There were few privacies, few family secrets in our household . . .

I was a very pretty child, and had a sweet voice . . . most London boys and girls of the lower classes sing. 'My face is my fortune, kind sir, she said', was the ditty on which I bestowed most pains, and my father and mother would wink knowingly as I sang it. The latter would also tell me how pretty she had been when young, and how she sang, and what a fool she had been, and how well she might have done had she been wise.

Frequently we had quite a stir in our colony. Some young lady who had quitted the paternal restraints . . . would appear among us with a profusion of ribands, fine clothes, and lots of cash. Visiting the neighbours, treating indiscriminately, was the order of the day on such occasions, without any more definite information of the means by which the dazzling transformation had been effected than could be conveyed by knowing winks and the words 'luck' and 'friends' . . . You cannot conceive, sir, how our ambition was stirred by these visitations . . .

Now commences an important era in my life. I was a fine, robust, healthy girl, 13 years of age. I had larked with the boys of my own age. I had huddled with them, boys and girls together, all night long in our own common haunts . . . For some time I had coquetted on the verge of a strong curiosity, and a natural desire, and without a particle of affection . . . I lost – what? not my virtue, for I never had any. That which is commonly, but untruly called virtue, I gave away. You reverend Mr Philanthropist – what call you virtue? . . . No such principle ever kept watch and ward over me, and I repeat that I never lost that which I never had – my virtue.

According to my own ideas at the time I only extended my rightful enjoyments. Opportunity was not long wanting to put my newly acquired knowledge to profitable use. In the commencement of my fifteenth year one of our be-ribbanded visitors took me off, and introduced me to the great world, and thus commenced my career as what you better classes call a prostitute. I cannot say that I felt any other shame than the bashfulness of a noviciate introduced to strange society. Remarkable for good looks, and no less so for good temper, I gained money, dressed gaily, and soon agreeably astonished my parents and old neighbours by making a descent upon them.

Passing over the vicissitudes of my course, alternating between reckless gaiety and extreme destitution, I improved myself greatly; and at the age of 18 was living partly under the protection of one who thought he discovered that I had talent, and some good qualities as well as beauty, who treated me more kindly and considerately than I had ever before been treated, and thus drew from me something like a feeling of regard . . . under the protection of this gentleman, and encouraged by him, I commenced the work of my education; that portion of education which is comprised in some knowledge of my own language and the ordinary accomplishments of my sex. . . .

Now, what if I am a prostitute, what business has society to abuse me? Have I received any favours at the hands of society? If I am a hideous cancer in society, are not the causes of the disease to be sought in the rottenness of the carcass? . . . what has society ever done for me, that I should do anything for it, and what have I ever done against society, that it should drive me into a corner and crush me to the earth? I have neither stolen (at least since I was a child), nor murdered, nor defrauded. I earn my money and pay my way, and try to do good with it, according to my ideas of good. I do not get drunk, nor fight, nor create uproar in the streets or out of them . . . I pay business visits to my tradespeople, the most fashionable of the West End. My milliners, my silk mercers, my bootmakers, know, all of them, who I am and how I live, and they solicit my patronage as earnestly and cringingly as if I were Madam, the Lady of the right rev. patron of the Society for the Suppression of Vice. They find my money good and my pay better (for we are robbed on every hand) than that of Madam, my lady; and, if all the circumstances and conditions of our lives had been reversed, would Madam, my lady, have done better or been better than I? . . .

Like 'One more unfortunate', there are other intruders among us – a few, very few, 'victims of seduction'. But seduction is not the root of the evil – scarcely a fibre of the root. A rigorous law should be passed and rigorously carried out to punish seduction, but it will not perceptibly thin the ranks of prostitution. Seduction is the common story of numbers of well brought up, who never were seduced. Vanity and idleness send us a large body of recruits. Servant girls, who wish to ape their mistresses' finery, and whose wages won't permit them to do so honestly – these set up seduction as an excuse. Married women, who have no respect for their husbands, and are not content with their lawful earnings, these are the worst among us . . .

'One more unfortunate' proposes a skimming process. But what of the great bubbling cauldron? Remove from the streets a score or two of 'foreign women' and 'double as many English' and you diminish the competition of those that remain . . . you 'miss' the evil, but it is existent still. After all, it is something to save the eye from offence, so remove them; and not only a score or two, but something like two hundred foreign women, whose open and disgusting indecencies and practices have contributed more than anything else to bring on our heads the present storm of indignation. It is rare that English women, even prostitutes, give cause of gross public offence. Cannot they be packed off to their own countries with their base, filthy and filthy-living men whom they maintain, and clothe, and feed, to superintend their fortunes, and who are a still greater disgrace to London than these women are?

Hurling big figures at us, it is said that there are 80,000 of us in London alone – which is a monstrous falsehood – and of those 80,000, poor hardworking sewing girls, sewing women, are numbered in by thousands, and called indiscriminately prostitutes; writing, preaching, speechifying, that they have lost their virtue too.

It is a cruel calumny to call them in mass prostitutes; and as for their virtue, they lose it as one loses his watch who is robbed by the highway thief. Their virtue is the watch, and society is the thief. These poor women toiling on starvation wages, while penury, misery and famine clutch them by the throat and say 'Render up your body, or die'.

Admire this magnificent shop in this fashionable street; its front, fittings, and decorations cost no less than a thousand pounds. The respectable master of the establishment keeps his carriage and lives in his country-house. He has daughters too; his patronesses are fine ladies, the choicest impersonations of society. Do they think, as they admire the taste and elegance of that tradesman's show, of the poor creatures who wrought it, and what they were paid for it? Do they reflect on the weary toiling fingers, on the eyes dim with watching, on the bowels yearning with hunger, on the bended frames, on the broken constitutions, on poor human nature driven to its coldest corner and reduced to its narrowest means in the production of these luxuries and adornments? This is an old story! Would it not be truer and more charitable to call these poor souls 'victims'? – some gentler, some more human name than prostitute – to soften by some Christian expression if you cannot better the un-Christian system, the opprobium of a fate to which society has driven them by the direst straits? What business has society to point its finger in scorn? . . .

Sir, I have trespassed on your patience beyond limit, and yet much remains to be said. . . . The difficulty is for society to set itself, with the necessary earnestness, self-humiliation and self-denial, to the work. To deprive us of proper and harmless amusements, to subject us in mass to the pressure of force – of force wielded, for the most part, by ignorant and often brutal men – is only to add the cruelty of active persecution to the cruelty of passive indifference which made us what we are.

I remain, your humble servant,

'Another Unfortunate'

The editor of *The Times* continued the discussion, calling the letter a revelation.

The Times, *25 February 1858*

The Great Social Evil, as it is not unfairly called, will remain a problem in our time. . . . We acknowledge, and we deplore its existence, but we know of no remedy which would not rather aggravate than soften the evil . . . We cannot import this offence as a crime into our Penal Code. It must be left almost entirely to private feeling; indeed, all that we can do is insist, on the part of the public, that outward decency be preserved. We do not believe that it is necessary to the preservation of our liberties that our most crowded thoroughfares should be daily and nightly paraded by some scores of gross foreign women, interspersed with a sprinkling of the most shameless among our own countrywomen. The persons of which we speak are just as well known to the police as the most advanced practitioners of the swell mob, and could readily be removed without possibility of mistake or oppression. Their presence in our principal streets is a standing nuisance. Why should it be tolerated that any of us cannot take mother or wife, sister or daughter, for a walk in Regent Street, or pass them in and out of a theatre or other place of public amusement, without being compelled to bring them into contact with what they had better not see? . . .

. . . We should like to know who would be injured by the removal of some couple of hundred of gross and notorious prostitutes from our chief thoroughfares? The wretched Frenchwomen who infest Regent Street are, as we are informed by a correspondent whose letter we inserted yesterday in this journal, in most instances jobbed upon by men who live upon the earnings . . . To these wretches, of course, the break up of the system would operate as a serious discouragement and a heavy loss.

Let the streets, then, especially the principal thoroughfares, be purged of this nuisance. It is, however, but reasonable to ask that respectable neighbourhoods shall not be annoyed by the existence of houses among them which may cause public scandal. Upon this point the public again have a right to step in . . . if the nighthouses be brought into the same orderly condition as the ordinary public houses, and if some restraint be placed upon the introduction of young girls from Hamburg, Belgium, France etc, for the purposes of prostitution, we know not that any more can be attempted without an aggravation of the evil which we would gladly see diminished . . .

We have never been hopeful upon the subject, but what little expectation one might have entertained was sadly dashed by the letter of the correspondent to which we have already alluded. The writer is, we entirely believe, what she professes to be – 'Another Unfortunate'. We are not endeavouring to palm off a cunningly executed literary imposture upon our readers. The letter is, to the best of our belief, a revelation of the feelings of the class to which the writer openly declares that she belongs. Now, the singularity of the communication consists of this – that the writer, who must be supposed to be tolerably well acquainted with the feelings of her associates and friends – bids us, in considering the subject, to dismiss from our apprehension all the crudities with which divines, and philanthropists, and romance writers have surrounded it. The great bulk of the London prostitutes are not Magdalens either in *esse* or *posse*, nor specimens of humanity in agony, nor Clarissa Harlowes. They are not – the bulk of them – cowering under gateways, nor preparing to throw themselves from Waterloo bridge, but are comfortably practising their trade, either as the entire or partial means of their subsistence. To attribute to them the sentimental delicacies of a heroine of romance would be equally preposterous. They have no remorse or misgivings about the nature of their pursuit; on the contrary, they consider the calling an advantageous one, and they look on their success in it with satisfaction. They have their virtues, like others; they are good daughters, good sisters, and friends, at least proportionately so with other classes of the community . . .

This is certainly a new view of the 'Great Social Evil', and worthy of the attention of all persons who are endeavouring to deal with it in a more complete manner than we can venture to recommend in the present state of our knowledge. But even the writer of this remarkable letter does not ask that the common decency shall be violated with impunity in our public streets: 'After all', she says, 'it is something to save the eye from offence; so remove, not only a score or two, but something like 200 foreign women, whose open indecencies and practices have contributed more than anything else to bring on our heads the present storm of indignation.' At least it would be worth while to do this, before having recourse to any more stringent measures. The thing might be tried by the simple issue of a direction to the police, amid the very general applause of the community.

Arthur Munby (1828–1910), upper class poet and civil servant, was one of the most curious men of Victorian Britain. Outwardly a conventional, Cambridge-educated member of the London professional classes, he was privately a man obsessed by working class women, an obsession which led him to secretly marrying a female servant, Hannah Cullwick. For most of his adult life he spent much of his spare time stopping and interviewing working class women in the streets of London and provincial towns. Like Gladstone he had an abiding interest in prostitutes, but unlike Gladstone he made no attempt to rescue them. Instead he recorded his interviews in his voluminous diaries. Through his diaries, we have an unusual opportunity to view street life, and hear the voices of street women, from a source which had no overt missionary purpose. The following extracts are taken from Munby's diaries of 1859, when he was lecturing at the Working Men's College set up by the Christian Socialist F.D. Maurice and when he was intimate with the famous publisher Alexander Macmillan, the art critic John Ruskin and other Victorian literati.

The Munby Diaries

Thursday 17th February. In the evening my class at the W M College. Afterwards went with Litchfield[1] to Macmillan's in Henrietta Street. Had supper, pipes & long tête-à-tête with Macmillan[2] on various subjects, eg 'Out of the Depths',[3] the biography of a prostitute, by a young parson – a plain outspoken healthful book, it seems, which with judicious boldness he is bringing out: the Burns business; and old Maurice . . . However obscure these may be to such as only understand, & do not feel, it is quite pleasant to see what an influence they have on men who, with clear heads, have also sound loving hearts. . . .

Sunday 20th March. Breakfasted with Litchfield, Ormsby being there also. Talk chiefly of comparative morality of this generation and the last, and of the advantage or otherwise of repressing street vice: as to which on the whole I side against the puritans, & am in favour of the unmolested street walker – provided she be sober, well dressed and not too importunate. It is certain, as Ormsby said, that the clearance, so called, of the Haymarket and the Casinos produced a large and still flourishing crop of secret dens & night haunts all about . . .

Sunday 10th April. . . . In the afternoon I walked up to Kilburn.[4] On my way home, being importuned by a girl in the Strand to come home with her, I replied by way of excuse 'but it's Sunday'; on which she exclaimed 'What, are you so froom as all that?' – '*Froom*' she explained, meant religious; but query the word, which is new to me.

Thursday 2nd June. . . . I walked home about 4am; broad daylight. The street scenes at that hour, especially at the top of the Haymarket, were quite Hogarthian. The last stragglers were just reeling out of the 'Pic'[5] & talking or squabbling outside: two gentlemen in evening dress, a few unwashed foreigners, several half-drunken prostitutes, one of whom, reeling away, drops her splendid white bonnet in the gutter, & another dances across the street, showing her legs above the knee: languid waiters in shirt sleeves stand looking on from their doors; two or three cabmen doze on the box behind their dozing horses: and a ragged beggarwoman skulks along in the shadow of the houses. Beyond them all . . . stands with dead calm face the Rhadamanthine peeler . . .

Saturday 30th July. . . . Going to the Opera, I met in the Strand one Sarah Tanner, who in 1854 or 5 was a maid of all work to a tradesman in Oxford Street; a lively honest rosy-faced girl, virtuous and self possessed. A year or so after, I met her in Regent Street, arrayed in gorgeous apparel. How is this? said I. Why, she had got tired of service, wanted to see life and be independent; and so she had become a prostitute, of her own accord and without being seduced. She saw no harm in it; enjoyed it very much, thought it might raise her & perhaps be profitable. She had taken it up as a profession, & that with much energy; she had read books, and was taking lessons in writing and other accomplishments in order to fit herself to be a companion of gentlemen . . .

During the next two or three years I saw her twice or thrice at intervals on duty, and generally stopped to talk. She was always well but not gaudily dressed; always frank and rosy and pleasant; and never importunate; nor did I ever hear her say a vicious word. . . .

After this I never saw her till tonight, when I met her in the Strand . . . dressed not professionally as a 'lady' but quietly & well, like a respectable upper servant . . . 'Married?' I asked. 'Oh no! But I'd been on the streets for three years, and saved up . . . I've taken a coffee house with my earnings – the Hampshire Coffeehouse, over Waterloo Bridge'. I laughed, incredulous. 'Quite true', said she simply, 'I manage it all myself, & can give you chops and tea – and anything you like; you must come and see me.' 'That I will', said I; for her manner was so open and businesslike that I saw it was true; and with a friendly goodbye we parted.

Now here is a handsome young woman of twenty-six, who, having begun life as a servant of all work, and then spent three years in voluntary prostitution amongst men of a class much above her own, retires with a little competence, and invests the earnings of her infamous trade in a respectable coffeehouse . . . That the coffeehouse is respectable is clear I think from her manner; that she did invest her earnings in it I believe, because she was not fashionable enough to be pensioned, & if she were, men do not pension off their whores in that way. Surely then this story is a singular contribution to the statistics of the 'Social Evil' and of female character and society in the lower classes.

The debate on street prostitution petered out in the early 1860s. Pressure from the anti-vice campaigners for action failed to move the government, and Cyril Pearl in *Girl with the Swansdown Seat* suggests (pp. 47–8) that they fell out among themselves. The correspondence in *The Times* petered out into an absurd argument about street nuisances in January 1862. By this time it was clear that no action would be taken against street prostitution, and that its opponents could do little more than fulminate against what most opinion formers saw as an inconvenience rather than a major problem. The real debate had already moved elsewhere, particularly to the argument about the impact of venereal disease on the military.

1.   Richard Buckley Litchfield (1832–1903), barrister and founder member of Working Man's College.
2.   Alexander MacMillan (1818–1906) held weekly 'tobacco parliaments' for congenial literary men, in his publishing firm's office.
3.   *Out of the Depths: the Story of a Woman's Life*, Anon. but by Henry Gladwyn Jebb.
4.   Hannah was then in service in Kilburn.
5.   The Piccadilly, a supper house.

5. The Pretty Horse Breakers: Upper Class Vice in the Spotlight

In the 1860s a new dimension was added to the discussion of prostitution in Britain, with a brief but intense scrutiny of upper class vice. Street prostitution and brothels were used by men of all social classes, but the keeping of mistresses was the province of rich men, largely ignored by public opinion since the Regency. In that era, the use of mistresses had been a standing insult to respectability. The scandal became notorious with the career of Harriett Wilson. This high class whore was patronised by three dukes – Wellington, Leinster and Argyll – several other peers and three sons of peers including the Marquess of Worcester and Lord Frederick Lamb. Before she published her memoirs, she offered several of her lovers the chance to be expunged from her reminiscences – for the price of £200 each. Several complied, but the most famous, the Duke of Wellington, responded with the famous response 'publish and be damned'. Which she did, producing four volumes of memoirs in 1825.

Thereafter, high class prostitutes disappeared into the shadows, though the informed knew very well where they could be found. However, they were not the subject of public debate till the end of the 1850s, when their widespread visibility on the arms of rich men at respectable entertainments became a matter for comment. 'There can be no disguising the fact', said a writer in *Paul Pry* in 1857, 'that at the West End, at Brompton, at St John's Wood, Foley Place, Portland Road, Regent's Park, and intermediate spots some of the most magnificent women in London live under the protection of gentlemen.'

However, the most distressing aspect of the situation for respectable opinion was the open visibility of these women in Hyde Park. Any attractive woman who could ride was allowed to enter the Park on horseback although she would have been denied access on foot. This allowed the *demi-monde*, as they were called – the English language had no way of describing courtesans beyond the half-hearted euphemism of 'pretty horse breakers' for the women who rode in Rotten Row – to meet rich men who otherwise would have been beyond their reach.

Writing in 1859, George Augustus Sala rejoiced. 'Can any scene in the world

An afternoon ride in Hyde Park. (Engraving by Gustave Doré. Mansell Collection)

equal Rotten Row at four in the afternoon and in the full tide of the season? Watch the sylphides as they fly or float past in their ravishing riding habits and intoxicatingly delightful hats; some with the orthodox cylindrical beaver, with the flowing veil; others with rogueish little wide-awakes, or pertly cocked cavalier's hats and green plumes. And as the joyous cavalcade streams past . . . from time to time the naughty wind will flutter the skirt of a habit, and display a tiny, coquettish brilliant little boot, with a military heel, and tightly strapped over it the Amazonian riding trouser.'

The situation even gave rise to a music hall song, with the refrain:

> The young swells in Rotten Row, All cut it mighty fine,
> And quiz the fair sex, you know, and say it is divine,
> The pretty little horsebreakers are breaking hearts like fun,
> For in Rotten Row they all must go, The whole hog or none,

which was more accurate than poetical.

The situation outraged respectable opinion, and in July 1860 the *Morning Post* published an attack on these doings as being worse than the looseness of the Regency. This was republished in *The Times,* and the more cynical *Saturday Review* commented that even 'patrician maidens' referred to the matter without shame. Matters came to a head in 1861 when the leading courtesan of the day, Catherine Walters, was celebrated in a portrait by Sir Edwin Landseer. 'The Taming of the Shrew' was the Picture of the Year. It was said to be a portrait of a chaste horsewoman, Miss Gilbert, but bore little resemblance to her and few cosmopolitans had any doubt that this was a portrait of Catherine Walters, better known by her nickname 'Skittles'. By far the most attractive of the courtesans in Rotten Row, from 1859 to 1863 Skittles enjoyed an increasingly notorious relationship with Lord Hartington, later 8th Duke of Devonshire. The liaison between the most eligible bachelor in London and an ex-Liverpool prostitute would provide the biggest scandal of 1862. But in 1861 the portrait of Skittles was the issue, provoking a pointed debate via the following letter to *The Times,* ostensibly from 'Seven Belgravian Mothers', but probably from James Matthew Higgins, man about town and a quixotic provoker of controversies.

'A Belgravian Lament', letter to The Times, *27 June 1861*

Sir – We, seven Belgravian mothers appeal to you . . . to make known our present distressing condition . . . We are mothers – with one exception, noblewomen . . . we have all without exception daughters at our disposal, of

Catherine Walters ('Skittles'). (Mary Evans Picture Library)

whom we have now for several seasons, industriously and in all propriety endeavoured to dispose. To make them eligible as wives of high rank we spared no pains, no cost, no amount of careful study. They were carefully reared at our country seats in every principle, that we, and religious governesses at high salaries, esteemed to be good. They have had the fullest advantages the best masters could afford to perfect their accomplishment in everything which 'society' expects in young ladies of this advanced day . . .

We have taken every advantage – some of us – of at least seven seasons, and yet our dear girls are still at home. We cannot accuse ourselves of any neglect of our duty, as mothers with one purpose at heart – their establishment as wives; we have ever diligently sought their attachment, as far as Providence permitted us, to the 'heirs' of the day. Balls, bazaars, breakfasts, concerts, scientific conversazioni, the churches and chapels, where music, art, or eloquence attract the young men of the day; the Opera, Epsom, Ascot, Volunteer reviews, even the Crystal Palace – all of these gave us opportunities. No one can say we ever neglected them or misused them . . . from day to night, night to day, we have worked for our daughters, but all has been in vain.

We seven have at this moment 24 daughters, actually what our sons call 'in running', not one of whom has had an offer that any one of us mothers for a moment could have seriously entertained . . . However unpleasant, indelicate the truth, all dreadful as it is to us to write it, marriage in our set is voted a bore – is repudiated . . .

With all pain, and some shame, we declare it, – an openly recognised anti-matrimonial element pervades good society . . . And why? Because what our simple-minded daughters call 'the pretty horse-breakers' occupy naughtily and temporarily where we should occupy *en permanence*.

Go where we will, the mother's eye has this social cruel pest intruded upon it; these bad rivals of our children are no longer kept in the background, as things we know, but, knowing, are seen not to know. Neither Row nor ring, church nor chapel, opera nor concert are wanting in their evident presence. . . . Time was, Sir, when a Lawrence, and then a Grant, placed on the walls of the Royal Exhibition lovely pictures each season of daughters now first offered to the attention of England's fashionable world – pretty advertisments of our pretty, chaste wares. That day seems for ever gone. The picture of the year is a 'Pretty Horse-Breaker' – but too well known – by Sir E. Seaview, RA.

Now, Sir, do tell us, are we to blame? Is it our fault? It is hinted that we have connived at and foster this evil . . . that we have made such a poor affectation of blindness that it was accepted as proof that we condoned, and hence it is that those whom too late we have learned to hate have been intruded on our

A 'sporting horse breaker'. (*The Day's Doings*, vol. 2, 27 May 1871, p. 276. Mary Evans Picture Library)

society, and ride side by side with our daughters. It is said that . . . by making heavy settlements so imperative, we drove younger sons to the evil life which was comparatively cheap, seeing that they never could hope to support the expensive life of married propriety . . . Pray help us, Sir . . . The whole girl life of our order is in danger; the pretty confirmations at the Chapel Royal, the prettier ceremonies at St George's – alas! alas! And then the sin of it all!

'A Sorrowing Mother for Seven of Them'

This amusing letter made a number of accurate digs at real fears among the parents of respectable unmarried daughters. The expense of marriage was taken up by another correspondent (or Higgins using another pseudonym?) calling himself Beau Jolais, who argued 'Girls are now so expensively, thoughtlessly brought up, and led to expect so lavish an outlay on the part of the husband . . . that hundreds have been forced to abandon all notion of a connubial alliance.'

The following day the *Daily Telegraph* laughed *The Times* and its alleged correspondents to scorn.

Daily Telegraph, *28 June 1861*

It is not a very seemly spectacle to behold the members of a haughty and wealthy aristocracy indulging in pathetic lamentations . . . If we could place anything approaching belief in the genuineness of the epistle published yesterday by our contemporary *The Times*, and purporting to come from 'Seven Belgravian Mothers', we should sigh at the sad state of things . . . but we experience some little relief in the knowledge that the letter no more emanates from seven English noblewomen than it does from seven Irish washerwomen . . .

That girls in the uppermost ranks of life are frivolous, and vapid, and in many cases anything but desirable partners for a man who wants a woman and not a wax doll for his wife, is no new thing to be told. MR THACKERAY has written so over and over again in his admirable romances . . . If we were to go back to the novels of MRS MANLEY and PATTY FIELDING and APHRA BEHN, we should find the same opinions expressed in somewhat coarser language . . . So long as the young ladies of the aristocracy are taught only to dress themselves like popinjays . . . so long as what they term religion is a compound of devotional dram drinking, maudlin sentimentalising . . . and masquerade moppings and mowings in the Puseyite gimcrack shops – so long will we have squabbles about settlements, flirtations without love, marriages without regard for human feeling . . . all ending with an appeal to SIR RICHARD CRESSWELL, and a scandalous case in the Divorce Court.

As for the 'pretty horsebreakers', we cannot believe that it has become the habit of noble English matrons and their daughters to make the lives and adventures of disreputable women the theme of their conversation. There is no harm in being aware of their existence. It would be the vilest hypocrisy in any woman, however highly placed she might be, to affect ignorance of their condition and mode of life . . . we draw no invidious distinction between the 'pretty horsebreakers' and their sisters of the *pavé*; for where one artful or lucky woman in a hundred may persuade some rich old idiot or some scatterbrain peer to make her his wife, the vast majority accomplish the full curriculum of

'*Rose-leaf crumples.*'

Edith. "Oh dear! I am so tired!"

Loving Husband. "What has fatigued you, my pippetywippety poppet?"

Edith. "Oh! I have had to hold up my parasol all the time I was in the carriage!"

(*Punch*, 6 May 1876. Reproduced with permission of Punch Ltd)

the Harlot's Progress. From the house at St John's Wood, the brougham and pair, the diamonds, the gay parties and gayer suppers, to Regent Street and the Strand, the gin shop and the kennel, there are very few steps indeed; and for one painted vanity, who has been 'made an honest woman of', how many haggard, ragged wretches, cowering in corners and crouching on doorsteps, will dilate with hoarse voices on the days when they were in 'the best of keeping' and had carriages, and horses, and servants, and jewels, and cashmere shawls. The daughters of the aristocracy need fear little from these forlorn competitors . . .

Everyone who is really familiar with English society knows that its tone is infinitely purer than it was a century ago; that men of quality would be

ashamed to pay the open court to abandoned women which was once paid
to MISS REAY, to HARRIETTE WILSON, and to MARY ANNE CLARKE; and
that no English sovereign would dare to enoble a courtesan as GEORGE I
enobled Mademoiselle DE SCHUYLEMBURG and GEORGE II, Madame
WALMODEN. If the figments of *The Times* have indeed a foundation in truth
. . . all we can say is that we are very concerned to hear it . . . the evidence
of our own eyes convinces us that in the course of time good, virtuous and
amiable girls find husbands without any trouble. If marriage is totally to die
out among the ineffables, such a solution of aristocratic continuity would
have its compensations in the extinction of a very vicious, frivolous and
useless class.

This robust defence of a healthy moral state was quickly abandoned. By December,
the editorial columns of the *Daily Telegraph* carried the following lament for the
passing of respectable marriage. The tone of near despair is unmistakable, but it is
not backed with real evidence.

Daily Telegraph, *13 December 1861*

There are some stories which never grow old. One of them is the story is Circe,
who reigned . . . over a beautiful island, inviting passing mariners to bring to in
the green harbour, and partake of her pleasures and banquets. But when the
fatal goblets were once tasted, the manhood of her guests straightway left them.
Transformed into swine, into dogs and into sheep, they grunted and howled
and bleated around her domains . . . But when the hero comes to the
treacherous palace . . . He draws his bright Greek sword upon the enchantress,
and, by virtue of his chastity alone, saves himself . . . The Circe of our day is
just as fair, and just as fatal. Call her LUXURY or LUST, or what you will, she is
ever beckoning gallant ships aside from the voyage of life. She has her halls full
of fools, quaffing the poisoned wine of illicit pleasure and her styes crowded
with swine that were once men of fair hope and good fame . . .

   The Rev Mr Brock was therefore quite justified when, in the St James's Hall
on Wednesday last, he declared the time come for an exposure of the great sin
of our society. So surely can the physician, listening at the stethoscope, can catch
the muffled sound which means death, so certainly the philosopher and the
publicist may foretell the ruin of the country if the fatal tone at its heart cannot
be arrested. It means that marriage is being set aside, that lust is being written
for love, that fashion is compiling on sand a new version of the laws which God
wrote on stone . . .

Our journals are full of causes which shame the courts, our streets are full of a sad sisterhood whose misery will weigh us down like a millstone. Elegant writers do not blush to talk the slang of the 'demi-monde'; leading journals doubtfully balance the 'wife' with the 'horsebreaker', and a favourite opera employs the divine strains of music and the genius of great artists to make a consumptive harlot a fit spectacle for honest women. In circles to which the people look up it is voted slow to deserve a wife by chastity, and to keep a wife by manly work, which God's law and natures enjoin . . . The correct thing now is a boudoir at Brompton or St John's Wood, and a caged bird in it, caught somewhere in the sweet meadows of womanhood, and tamed to sing in those gilded wires. For those who cannot reach this Paradise of fools there are other lower Heavens, other refuges from the distress of marriage . . . And this is the CIRCE that wrecks our English ships! This poor shore of drugged wine . . . is fair enough to our youth and to our manhood to win them aside from the voyage of life . . . They are not wholly won, in truth – they are partly driven. 'Belgravian mothers' are to blame, and the class they represent . . . those ill women who do not know that the love of an honest man is the one dowry to insist upon for a daughter. These share the sin that threatens us. To these as well as those the danger of the land is due. Restore, we bid them, to its place upon their list of merits the courage and the honour of a heart that has not sought its mate in the gutter, nor left one there.

Though emotion overpowers analysis here, the *Daily Telegraph* editorial reveals real fears about real developments. That the most notorious whore of the day should be hung in portrait at the Royal Academy was remarkable enough. The *Annual Register* commented primly, 'Unfortunately the picture was suggestive of one of the social scandals of the hour, and the public was as much attracted by "The Pretty Horse Breaker" as by the wonderful art of the painter.' And for those unaware of the nature of the scandal referred to, 1862 brought enlightenment.

In the summer of 1862 Hartington's affair with Skittles was highlighted when he was seen with her at the Derby. This was giving hostages to fortune, and in July the storm broke. *The Times* published another apparently innocent, tongue-in-cheek letter which had an even sharper edge than the missive from the Belgravian mothers.

'Anonyma': letter to The Times, *3 July 1862*

Sir: Early in the season of 1861 a young lady whom I must call 'Anonyma', for I have never been able to learn her name, made her appearance in Hyde Park.

She was a charming creature, beautifully dressed, and she drove with ease and spirit two of the handsomest brown ponies eye ever beheld.

Nobody in society had every seen her before; nobody in society knew her name, or to whom she belonged, but there she was, prettier, better dressed, and sitting more gracefully in her carriage than any of the fine ladies who envied her her looks, her skill or her equipage. . . .

Anonyma seemed at first to be rather a shy damsel. She is somewhat bolder now. That year she avoided crowds, and affected unfrequented roads, where she could more freely exhibit her ponies' marvellous action, and talk to her male acquaintances with more becoming privacy. . . .

But, as the fame of her beauty and her equipage spread, this privacy became impossible to her. The fashionable world eagerly migrated in search of her from the Ladies' Mile to the Kensington Road. The highest ladies in the land enlisted her as their disciples. Driving became the rage. . . . Where she drove, they followed; and I must confess that, as yet, Anonyma has fairly distanced her fair competitors. They can none of them sit, dress, drive or look as well as she does; nor can any of them procure for money such ponies as Anonyma contrives to get – for love.

But the result of all this pretty play causes a great public nuisance, and it is on this account, and not at all on account of my admiration for Anonyma and her stepping ponies, that I now address you.

. . . Up to the beginning of last year the fashionable world chiefly affected the Ladies' Mile in the Park . . . the thoroughfare from Apsley House to Kensington was comparatively unfrequented, save by Anonyma. But this year, when that road is more especially required to be kept open for the convenience of visitors to the Exhibition, it is daily choked with fashionable carriages – from five to seven – all on account of Anonyma. Chairs are placed along it either side; the best parties that England knows . . . all sit there watching for Anonyma. About 6pm a rumour arises that Anonyma is coming. Expectation rises to its highest pitch; a handsome woman drives rapidly by in a carriage drawn by thoroughbred ponies . . . but alas! she causes no effect at all, for she is not Anonyma; she is only the Duchess of A—, the Marchioness of B—, the Countess of C—, or some other of Anonyma's eager imitators. The crowd, disappointed, reseat themselves, and wait. Another pony carriage succeeds – and another – with the same depressing result. At last their patience is rewarded. Anonyma and her ponies appear, and they are satisfied. She threads her way decorously, with an unconscious air, through the throng, commented on by hundreds who admire and hundreds who envy her. She pulls up her ponies to speak to an acquaintance, and his carriage is instantly surrounded by a multitude; she turns and drives back again towards Apsley House, and then – away into the unknown world, nobodys knows whither. Meanwhile thousands returning from the Exhibition are intolerably delayed by the crowd collected to gaze on this pretty creature and her pretty ponies, and the efforts of Sir Richard Mayne and his police to keep the thoroughfare open are utterly frustrated.

Could you not, Sir, whose business is to know everything and everybody, and who possibly, therefore, may know Anonyma herself, prevail on her to drive in some other portion of the Park as long as the Exhibition lasts? If she will but consent to do this, the fashionable crowd will certainly follow her, and the road to the Exhibition will be set free for the use of the public.

I am, Sir, your obedient servant, H.

This was very funny and very pointed, but the publicity wrecked Skittles' relationship with Hartington. In August he left for a six-month visit to America, while Skittles fled to Ems in Germany. The relationship dragged on into 1863 but in the spring Hartington's father learned of the affair and by the summer it was over.

Skittles went on to pursue her career elsewhere, inspiring remarkable affection from figures as diverse as her lover Wilfred Scawen Blunt, and the almost inevitable platonic relationship with a fascinated Gladstone. The *demi-monde* continued to parade in Rotten Row, a fact deplored by the *Pall Mall Gazette* in 1869.

'The Ladies' Mile', Pall Mall Gazette, *16 April 1869*

Although up to this period of the season the people who ride or drive in the Row have not been distracted by any specially sensational ponies under the direction of anonymous ladies, questionable broughams and horsebreakers have even thus early appeared in Hyde Park in excess of the number with which the assemblage is usually enlivened. But it is not so much of this circumstance, however, that we now write . . . Until very recently there was no such thing as a demi-monde in London, using the term in its imperfect meaning . . . but within a very brief period – not much more than a year perhaps – there has been a change among us. Previous to that time, indeed, moralists in the press complained of the frank terms which young men of fashion held [sic] with such women in places of public resort. This familiarity is now so much on the increase . . . that it calls for some remonstrance . . .

At present the yellow chignoned denizens of St John's Wood and Pimlico draw up their carriages or horses close to the rails, and are chatted with as candidly as if they had come from some dovecot in the country watched over by a virtuous mother. The audacity of these *reunions* is unprecedented. A notion seems to prevail that the loose women of our own day are indistinguishable from the women of virtue. The superstition is preposterous. In the Park, at least, there is no difficulty in guessing the occupation of the dashing equestrienne . . . who salutes half a dozen men at once with her whip or with a wink . . . Of course the men who talk with these women of the highway are perfectly well aware of what they are about, and a London lady tempered in the atmosphere of one or two seasons learns discretion enough not to ask relevant questions when she meets in a ballroom the same gentleman she has observed tête-à-tête with Aspasia in the Row. If things go on, however, as they seem likely to, this sort of reserve will be tested with unusual severity in the months of May and June . . .

William Acton republished this passage in the 1870 edition of his book *Prostitution*, and his comment on it is worth noting.

Prostitution, *1870*

I appeal with confidence to everyone acquainted with London life, and ask if this statement is not strictly true? but in that case, what becomes of the notion that the mischief, if left to itself, will work out its own cure? . . . And so it comes to pass that men consider the sin as a thing that everybody practises, though nobody talks too much about it, until to abstain is looked upon almost as a mark of want of manhood . . . Now I say the time has arrived when serious men should give to prostitution serious thought. It can no longer be ignored. The evils attendant on it are too great and too much on the increase . . . Let us do what we can. The mischief that must always exist will have more or less intensity according as we regulate it, or leave it to itself . . . Let us assume a position at once more manly and more humane . . .

That position was the legalisation and regulation of prostitution on the Continental model. For the present, Acton's comment that 'nobody talks too much about it' rang true where upper class male indulgence was concerned. But prostitution in its lower class forms certainly did not disappear from view. And while upper class vice disappeared from polite conversation through the 1870s, it was to reappear with force in 1885 in the furore surrounding 'The Maiden Tribute of Modern Babylon'.

6. The Campaign for Legalisation

By the late 1850s, the gap between rhetoric and reality over prostitution was increasingly clear to thinking people. The puritans could exert enough pressure to secure temporary victories, particularly in closing individual brothels, but in the absence of a general police campaign, this simply moved the problem from one location to another. The government was deeply resistant to strengthening the law, and the puritans clearly lacked the muscle to challenge this resistance. The result was impasse. The puritans continued their crusade, but other interested parties came to the conclusion that the law was unenforceable and that regulation – or at least systematic toleration – should be attempted. The public health lobby, whose most eloquent polemicist was William Acton, called for legalisation and regulation.

The argument for regulation was, however, first put publicly by W.R. Greg in the *Westminster Review* in 1850. William Rathbone Greg was a conservative, who sympathised with the views of his brother-in-law, Walter Bagehot, and was friendly with de Tocqueville. While he shared the conventional assumptions of his age about prostitution, notably the inevitability of the harlot's fall, he was prepared to confront directly the existence of a phenomenon which most respectable Victorians preferred to ignore, and bravely protested at the abysmal treatment accorded prostitutes. His article was the first major penetration of this emotive subject into the reading matter of the literate middle classes.

First published in volume 53 of the *Westminster Review*, 1850, pp. 448–506, these extracts are from Keith Nield, *Prostitution in the Victorian Age*, Gregg International Publishers 1973. [eio]

pp. 448–50
There are some questions so painful and perplexing, that statesmen, moralists and philanthropists shrink from them by common consent. The subject to which the following pages are devoted, is one of these. Of all the social problems which philosophy has to deal with, this is, we believe, the darkest, the knottiest, and the saddest . . . Statesmen see the mighty evil lying on the main pathway of the world, and, with a groan of pity and despair, 'pass by on the

other side'. They act like the timid patient, who, fearing and feeling the existence of a terrible disease, dares not examine its symptoms . . .

It is from a strong conviction that this is not worthy behaviour on the part of those who aspire to guide either the actions or the opinions of others, that, after much hesitation, and many misgivings, we have undertaken to speak of so dismal and delicate a matter . . . it is a false and mischievous delicacy, and a culpable moral cowardice, which shrinks from the consideration of the great social vice of Prostitution, because the subject is a loathsome one . . . we have deliberately resolved to call attention to it, though we do so with pain, reluctance and diffidence.

And first – to preclude misrepresentation . . . we must show our colours by expressing our own feelings as to fornication . . . We look upon fornication . . . as the worst and lowest form of sexual irregularity, the most revolting to the unpolluted feelings, the most indicative of a *low* nature, the most degrading and sapping to the loftier life . . . Sexual indulgence, however guilty in its circumstances, however tragic in its results, is, when accompanied by love, a sin *according to nature*; fornication is a sin *against nature* . . . The peculiar guilt of prostitution consists, in our view of the matter, in its being *unnatural*; a violation of our truer instincts – not merely a frailty in yielding to them. On this matter, therefore, we feel at least as strongly as any divine can do.

In the second place, we feel called upon to protest against the manner in which prostitutes are almost universally regarded, spoken of, and treated in this country, as dishonouring alike to our religion and manhood. This iniquity pervades all classes, and both sexes. No language is too savage for these wretched women. They are outcasts, pariahs, lepers . . . They are kicked, cuffed, trampled on with impunity by everyone. Their oaths are seldom regarded in a court of justice, scarcely ever in a police court. They seem to be considered far more out of the pale of humanity than negroes on a slave plantation, or fellahs in a pasha's dungeon . . .

pp. 454–5

The career of these women is a brief one; their downward path a marked and inevitable one; and they know this well. They are almost never rescued; escape themselves they cannot . . . The swindler may repent, the drunkard may reform; society aids and encourages them in their thorny path of repentance and atonement . . . But the prostitute may not pause, may NOT recover; at the very first halting, timid step she may make to the right or to the left, with a view to flight from her appalling doom, the whole resistless influences of the surrounding world, the good as well as the bad, close around her to hunt her back into perdition . . .

pp. 457–9

The causes which lead to the fall of women are various; but all of them are of a nature to move grief and compassion rather than indignation and contempt, in all minds cognizant of the strange composition of humanity . . . The first, and perhaps the largest class of prostitutes are those who may fairly be said to have had no choice in the matter – who were born and bred in sin; whose parents were thieves and prostitutes before them; whose dwelling has always been in an atmosphere of squalid misery and sordid guilt . . . Such abound in London, in Dublin, in Glasgow; and, though to a less extent, in all large towns . . . How this class is to be checked, controlled, diminished and finally extirpated, is one of the most difficult practical problems for English statesmen . . . but it is one with which, at present, we have not to do. All that we wish to urge is that the prostitutes who spring from this class, are clearly the victims of circumstances, and therefore must on all hands [sic] be allowed to be objects of the most unalloyed compassion.

Others, unquestionably, and alas! too many, fall from the snares of vanity . . . They enjoy the present pleasures, think they can secure themselves from being led on too far, and, like foolish moths, flutter around the flame which is to dazzle and consume them. For these we have no justification. . . . Still, even these are not worthy of the treatment they meet with, even from those of their own sex . . . Let those who are without sin among us, cast the first stone at them.

Some, too, there are for whom no plea can be offered – who voluntarily and deliberately sell themselves to shame, and barter in a cold spirit of bargain, chastity and reputation for carriages, jewels and a luxurious table. All that can here be urged is the simple fact . . . that in this respect the unfortunate women who ultimately come upon the town are far from being the chief, or the most numerous delinquents. For one woman who thus, of deliberate choice, sells herself to a lover, ten sell themselves to a husband . . . The barter is as naked and cold in the one case as in the other; the thing bartered is the same; the difference between the two transactions lies in the price that is paid down . . .

p. 461

We shall not take much pains in proving that poverty is the chief determining cause which drives women into prostitution in England, as in France; partly because we have no adequate statistics, and we are not disposed to present our readers with mere fallacious estimates, but mainly because no one doubts the proposition. Granting all that can be said of the idleness, extravagance and love of dress of these poor women, the number of those who would adopt such a life, were any other means of obtaining an adequate maintenance open to them, will be allowed on all hands to be small indeed. But we are particularly desirous to direct attention to some evidence recently laid before the public in Mr Mayhew's letters to the *Morning Chronicle*, as to the severity of the distress which daily drives many well disposed and otherwise well educated women to this disastrous and degrading resource . . .

pp. 468–9

The mode, however, in which, among the working classes, poverty most directly leads to loss of chastity, and ultimate prostitution, is common to all occupations and to all parts of the country; to the rural districts even more than the towns. We allude to . . . insufficient house accommodation. . . . Such is the state of the cottages inhabited by the labouring people that, however large the family, they have seldom more than one bedroom, never more than two. Married couples, grown up children of both sexes, cousins, and even lodgers, occupy the same room, where the bedding is often insufficient, and the proximity necessarily close. The consequences may be easily imagined – more easily than described. The evidence on this point is frightful and overwhelming. . . .

'In Hull,' (says Mr R. Wood), 'I have met with a mother fifty years of age, and her son above twenty-one, sleeping in the same bed and a lodger in the same room . . . I have met with instances of a man, his wife, and his wife's sister, sleeping in the same bed together. . . . I have frequently met with instances in which the parties themselves have traced their own depravity to these circumstances. For example, I found in one room in Hull a prostitute; and on asking the cause of her being brought to her present condition, she stated that she had lodged with a married sister, and slept in the same bed with her and her husband; that hence improper intercourse took place, and from that time she gradually became more and more depraved, until at length the town was her only resource . . . '

pp. 476–7

One of the most important practical points connected with this painful subject, is the deplorable extent and virulence of disease which prostitution is the means of spreading throughout the community. . . . The amount of social evil arising from syphilitic maladies, statistics cannot measure, even if trustworthy statistics were within our reach, which they are not. All that we know with certainty is, that the Lock Hospitals (those devoted to syphilitic patients) throughout the country are always full, and generally insufficient. One witness affirms that not one man in ten goes through life without being diseased at one point or another of his career. We do not believe this

'The Haunted Lady', or 'The Ghost in the looking Glass'. This pictures illustrates all too clearly the gulf between upper class and working class women. (*Punch*, 4 July 1863)

statement; but we do know that the disease prevails to an extent that is perfectly appalling . . . It must not be imagined that the mischief of syphilis can be measured even by the number of those who are ostensibly its victims . . . We must take into account the sufferings of those innocent individuals in private life who are infected through the sins of others; we must take into account the happiness of many families thus irretrievably destroyed; the thousands of children who are in consequence born into the world with a constitution incurably unsound; the certain, but incalculable deterioration of public health and of the vigour of the race, which must ensue in the course of a generation or two more . . .

pp. 478–9
Such being the evil we have to deal with, we now come to the practical and most painful questions – Can it be eradicated? – and if not, what can and

ought to be done to mitigate its mischief and diminish its amount? . . . Can prostitution be eradicated? – At present, per saltum and ab extra, certainly not. In a state of society like that which now prevails in England – with livelihood so difficult, and marriage so impeded by scantiness of means – with so many thousands constantly on the verge, and sometimes beyond the verge, of starvation, and whose urgent poverty will therefore overcome their reluctant wills – with idleness so prevalent among the rich, and education so defective among the poor . . . we fear that the extinction of the practice, or even its reduction from a rule to an exception, must be a most slow, gradual and incalculably difficult process . . .

pp. 481–6

We are prepared to concede that, as society is at present constituted, illicit intercourse will and must prevail to a very considerable extent; and from this, prostitution, we fear, must inevitably flow . . . But it is our firm conviction that, by looking the difficulty firmly in the face, this unhappy vice might be vastly diminished in degree, and the social evils which arise from it greatly mitigated in intensity. For example, there can be no doubt that it exists in France to at least as great an extent as with us, yet without being productive of nearly the same amount of mischief either to society, or to the unfortunate women themselves. Let us enquire whence this difference arises . . .

The prostitutes of Paris may be divided into three classes – those who are registered, and are in consequence under the protection and surveillance of the authorities; those who exercise their profession in too clandestine or too respectable a manner to come under the supervision of the police; and those wretches who swarm in the common lodging houses, and in those haunts of vice and squalor near the barracks and the outskirts of the city . . . It has, for a long period, been the chief aim of the administration to increase the first class at the expense of the two others, and toward this desirable end they are making slow but steady progress. They argue thus . . . By gradually drawing all prostitutes within the circle of our control, we can introduce regulations, and enforce checks on their proceedings, which will enable us to repress all more scandalous disorders, keep the evil within some limits, greatly promote the externals of decency, and materially diminish . . . the disease which now makes such grievous ravages . . .

On these principles they have now acted for many years . . . the number of prostitutes inscribed on the register of the *Bureau des Moeurs* increased from 1,300 in 1812, to 3,600 in 1832, and now considerably exceeds 4,000. These girls . . . are subject to the constant surveillance of authorised inspectors and medical men; certain rules of behaviour are enforced upon them . . . and they are subject to frequent periodical visits . . . from an appointed physician, who, if he finds them diseased, at once withdraws their certificate (for practicising without which, they are liable to arbitrary arrest) . . .

The benefit to public health which has resulted from the administrative measures that have been pursued, may be imagined from these two facts; upwards of 1,000 girls annually are arrested in the exercise of their profession, in consequence of syphilitic symptoms, and sent by authority into the hospital, where they are sequestered till their complete recovery is certified. Had it not been for this precaution, these girls would have continued to spread disease around them, and might have infected thousands, both of the guilty and the innocent. The other fact is this; in the year 1812, when the present sanitary regulations were first introduced, the proportion of registered prostitutes found infected at the periodical visits of the medical inspector, was one in twenty – it is now reduced to one in thirty-four . . .

pp. 486–93

We have now placed before our readers the data necessary to enable them to follow us in the inquiry which will close this paper: Ought we to do anything, and what ought we to do, in England, to diminish prostitution, and mitigate the intensity of the evils which arise from it?

On two points all parties are agreed, and the law has ratified the decision of the public. The first of these is, that traders in prostitution – those who make it their occupation to collect and entrap victims for the lust of others – shall be punished with wholesome severity . . . The common law having been found insufficient to meet crimes of this sort, a very concise and peremptory Act of Parliament [the 1849 Act] was passed in the last session . . . All that is needed to give full effect to this enactment is, that public opinion shall be thoroughly inlisted in its behalf . . .

The second point upon which all are agreed is, that carnal connexion with children of tender years, WITH OR WITHOUT CONSENT, is a high crime and misdemeanour. On this subject, also, the law has spoken clearly; and by an enactment now some years old, a man charged with rape on the person of a child under thirteen years of age, cannot plead her consent in bar of judgement . . .

A third proposition, which meets with the consent of most sober thinkers on this painful subject is, that voluntary intercourse between parties of mature age, however immoral in itself, must not be interfered with, unless carried out in such a manner as to outrage public decency, or endanger public health. On this point, however, we are at issue with those closet moralists who think that prostitution is, in itself and in any form, a sin which calls for legal repression; and also with those societies, composed of most estimable men . . . who make it their object to suppress brothels wherever they can obtain sufficient evidence against them . . .

It is a common mistake with many excellent men, to suppose that, because any action is wicked and mischievous, it necessarily follows that it is desirable to proceed against it by legal means. . . . All experience has shown that you cannot, by enactment, prevent ANY demand from being met by an adequate supply . . . we are obliged to come to the conclusion that it is inadvisable, as a general rule, to adopt repressive measures against prostitution and fornication, when practised by persons of mature age; it remains to be considered whether this general rule ought not to be departed from when public decency is outraged, or the public health endangered . . .

If public health is an affair which at all merits the attention of the government . . . if the late movement of popular feeling in favour of sanitary measures be not wholly a mistake . . . if quarantine regulations against imported pestilence – if enforced cleanliness in times of cholera visitation – be justified and right, then the natural a priori, a foriori conclusion unquestionably is, that it is an imperative duty on the administrative authorities to take all needful and feasible measures to check the spread of a malady more general, more constantly present, and more terrible than all other epidemics . . . Let us therefore weigh dispassionately the objections commonly urged against any attempt to check and eradicate the spread of syphilitic poison . . . by such regulation and supervision of prostitutes as shall prevent them from practising their *metier* when diseased . . .

The first objection we shall dispose of very cavalierly. We are told that such supervision . . . would be an infringement on the liberty of the subject. To this we shall content ourselves with replying that, no law and no society recognises in individuals a degree of liberty incompatible with the welfare and the rights of others . . .

A second, and a more rational objection is, that the fear of the maladies communicated by prostitutes acts as a powerful motive in restraining men from frequenting them; that if fornication were attended with no risk to health, the young would indulge in it far more freely and unreservedly than they do at present . . . This, however, is scarcely language that will be held by any but mere recluse reasoners. For two hundred and fifty years, since the middle of the sixteenth century when this malady first appeared, prostitutes have been allowed to spread infection on all sides of them without control. Let us (argues M. Duchatelet)* read the history of this long period . . . we shall find that the

*Parent-Duchalet

fear of the most horrible consequences has never produced any effect in deterring men from fornication . . .

Finally, it is urged that the 'tacit sanction' given to vice by such a recognition of prostitution as would be involved in a system of supervision, registration, or license, would be a greater evil than all the maladies (moral and physical) which now flow from its unchecked prevalence. But let it be considered that by ignoring, we do not abolish it; we do not even conceal it; it speaks aloud; it walks abroad; it is a vice as patent and as well known as drunkenness; it is already 'tacitly sanctioned' by the mere fact of its permitted or connived at existence . . . By an attempt to regulate and control them, the authorities would confess nothing more that they already in act knowledge – viz., their desire to mitigate an evil which they have discovered their incompetency to suppress . . .

pp. 494–502

There can be no doubt that such a rectification of social anomalies – such as a general amelioration in our social condition, as should place the means of earning an ample livelihood by honourable industry within the reach of women of all classes, would at once remove one of the most prolific of those sources whence prostitutes are supplied . . . But the means by which such a result can be obtained, present far too wide a subject for us to enter upon here. Nor must we be too sanguine in anticipating a very great diminution of prostitution from this cause alone; for in the United States, where the sexes are equal in the eye of the law, and the means of an ample maintenance are within reach of all . . . we find the vice far from rare . . .

The details we have given in an earlier part of this paper will show how much might be done by better and ampler house accommodation for the poor . . . As long as both sexes herd together in bed rooms, the barriers of modesty will be broken down too early in life to admit of their acting as bulwarks of virtue when the day of temptation shall arrive. This is one of the channels into which public charity may be turned, with the greatest hope of good . . .

The common lodging houses of the metropolis, and of most great towns, are among the worst sinks of iniquity and nurseries of prostitution that exist. These should be brought at once under the control of the police, not for the sake of suppression, but of surveillance and regulation; in these cases, as in that of brothels, suppression merely means closer concealment and removal into worse localities . . .

Another measure, the urgency of which has been strongly forced upon our minds during the course of our enquiries, is the establishment throughout the

country of an adequate number of asylums for those poor girls who wish either
to escape from a life of prostitution, or to avoid having recourse to it . . .

We would recommend the appointment of a special department connected
with the Board of Health, whose duty it shall be – with due safeguard against
the abuse of their powers – to take all needful and feasible measures to prevent
the spread of syphilitic infection. What these measures should be, would be a
question demanding the most cautious and searching investigation. Probably
the first which would approve themselves would be the establishment by
authority of a sufficient number of Lock Hospitals, and the subjecting of all
prostitutes . . . to a periodical medical inspection, with the prompt
sequestration or removal to the hospital of all who were found to be diseased.
This measure might in time be followed up by extending the power of these
special officers to the arrest and imprisonment of all prostitutes who should be
found practising their occupation without certificate that they had undergone
such medical inspection. We purposely abstain from entering into any further
details as to the precautionary measures which the Department of Health
might find it necessary to adopt; the establishment of such a department being
the point on which the public is, in the first instance, called upon to decide . . .

The measures above indicated will, to a certain extent . . . mitigate the evil
of prostitution, and diminish the number of its victims; for anything beyond
mitigation we must trust to the slow operation of moral influences . . . Public
opinion . . . must undergo considerable modification and enlightenment,
before much diminution of prostitution can be looked for. Towards such
modification we have here contributed our mite.

By 1857 the *Lancet*, edited by Thomas Wakely MP, had become converted by the
argument for regulation, a position put in the following editorial of 7 November
1857. The views set out in the article were over-emotional, but the journal
represented a growing belief among medical reformers which was shared, less
rhetorically, by the *British Medical Journal*, that regulation of prostitution was
necessary for public health.

'Prostitution – the need for its reform', the Lancet, 7 November 1857

'This', said Mr Disraeli in a recent speech, 'I believe to be the the age of
statistical imposture', and an ex-Chancellor of the Exchequer should be no mean
authority on such a point. As concerns prostitution, the elaborate statistics
collected represent in only a faint degree the amount of evil it is doing. . . . Its
dimensions have been very accurately measured. We know, on the best authority,

that one house in sixty in London is a brothel, and one in every sixteen females (of all ages) is, de facto, a prostitute [sic. The editorial provides no evidence and seems to rely on Talbot.] Yet, startling though these figures appear . . . they convey but a feeble impression of the effects produced on Society by the mass of sanctioned wickedness thus represented . . . the sworn testimony of many witnesses in frequent trials proves that there is a strong undercurrent of licentiousness and immorality . . .

It is, however, amongst the middle classes . . . that the chief mischief is done by the evil that they are the most persistent in ignoring. The typical Pater-familias, living in a grand house near the park, sees his sons lured into debauchery, dares not walk with his daughters though the streets after nightfall, and is disturbed from his night-slumbers by the drunken screams and foul oaths of prostitutes reeling home with daylight. If he look [sic] from his window, he sees the pavement – his pavement – occupied by the flaunting daughters of sin, whose loud, ribald talk forces him to keep his casement closed. Yet he refuses to sanction any practical means for remedying the evil, or to lend his aid to its reform. He not only allows the dirt to accumulate . . . but scrupulously carries out the social code under which prostitution has so notably increased of late years . . .

The *Lancet* had badly overstated its case. By the following spring, it had switched from broad-brush attacks on prostitution per se, to narrowly focused discussion of the problems prostitution posed for the military. A viable argument for state action was beginning to emerge, and the magazine tapped into a debate within Whitehall on this very issue; a government commission had been appointed on 5 May 1857 'to inquire into the sanitary condition of the British Army' inspired by the military failures of the Crimean War. The *Lancet* commented on this in its edition of 20 February 1858. This was developed via an article on the impact of venereal disease on the military. Extracts from this article are given below.

'Prostitution: its medical aspects', the Lancet, *20 February 1858*

Necessity, under whatever pretence it be disguised, is the great determining cause of legislation . . . unchecked prostitution . . . [is] inflicting increasing evils, the full extent of which has hitherto been unrecognised. And if all the direct physical and moral results . . . are not sufficient to demonstrate the necessity for legislative interference, there yet remain other evils which more immediately affect the state; and that through a very susceptible part – the pocket.

Our soldiers and sailors are trained and supported solely that by their physical strength they may do the State some service. Therefore, impairment of a man's health constitutes, *pro tanto*, a bad bargain to the country, and represents the loss of so much money. Now, when we find that from 1830 to 1847 the number of soldiers annually diseased varied from 181 to 206 per 1,000 men, or in other words, that about one-fifth of the whole effective force in this country are yearly in hospital with venereal disease for a period of twenty-two days (as calculated by Dr Gordon), we may easily judge what is the loss sustained in this branch of the service alone.

If the course of the diseased 'femme publique' . . . be borne in mind, it is scarcely necessary to point out how glaring an instance of wasteful inconsistency the above figure represents. . . . If, in the pursuit of her miserable avocation, she infect only three soldiers, they are forthwith submitted to skilful treatment at the national charge, and cause a direct loss of between three and four pounds to the state . . . Had proper hospital room [sic] been provided for the woman, her treatment and cure would have scarcely cost a tithe of the sum which is . . . lost to the State through her being at large. The result of the physical evil on the latter class of persons even more forcibly shows the necessity for state interference . . .

We are past the day when criminals and maniacs were made a show. As regards society, the diseased woman is somewhat in the same position. It is expedient to get rid of her as a *diseased* woman as soon as possible, and therefore to avoid everything which should lead to any delay in her coming under treatment . . .

Outside the medical world, the *Saturday Review* was an eloquent advocate of state regulation, commenting on the controversy over the Argyll Rooms in its edition of 16 October 1858 (pp. 373–4).

'The Argyll Rooms', Saturday Review, *16 October 1858*

Public decency is in a difficulty, and it seems that the remedy is worse than the disease. We appear to be in that condition which the Roman historian has described as the vice of a falling State – we can neither endure our vices nor their cures. Last year, in a transport of indignation, we closed the Argyll Rooms because they were the focus and complex of all metropolitan vice. This year we open them because, on the whole, it is better that the vicious population should be brought together than that it should be let loose on society. There is antecedently much to be said for either view of the moral question. A whole cloud of evidence was brought, on the recent occasion of the proprietor of the Rooms applying for a license, to show that the streets have been in a worse state since the lorettes of London were deprived of their customary home, than when they had a local habitation . . .

Evidence was tendered that the Argyll Rooms were frequented by respectable tradesmen and their wives. Five or six hundred noblemen and gentlemen are said to have offered, or to have been ready to offer, their testimony to the admirable way in which the Rooms were conducted. The music is of the most scientific character, order and decorum find their chosen home in Windmill Street, and the evidence at least suggests that Casinos divide with the pulpit the duty of preserving the general social health of London.

This is proving a little too much. Had the argument confined itself to the one simple ground that immorality must be, and that on the whole immorality and its haunts should be, under decent and responsible management and control, we own to a growing conviction that it was right to grant the license – not because the Argyll Rooms are a moral institution, but because, so long as they are open under the care and responsibility of a respectable, or at least substantial person, public morality suffers less than when harlotry unattached turns a whole quarter of London to an unlicensed Argyll Rooms and something worse . . .

To talk of prohibiting prostitution and the like is absurd. What there is left for the State is to deal with this and other social evils so as to render them less generally noxious. By dishonestly affecting to deny their existence, we commit an offence not only against truth, but also against policy. The State is not a God, whose eyes are too pure to behold iniquity . . . [it] must deal with facts and society as they are. It may be quite right for an individual . . . to take all consequences, and, instead of doing the least of two evils, to do no evil, whatever good may come of it. But the state is not an individual – it must provide the greatest good for the greatest number, and often this may only be by taking the least of two evils . . . If it cannot prohibit prostitution, its first duty is to make the best of it. We have made the worst of it by the impolicy of affecting not to see it.

If, therefore, we are to accept the licensing of the Argyll Rooms as a public recognition of vice to the extent of placing it under public control, . . . we should be disposed to accept with some satisfaction the decision of the Middlesex magistrates. What can't be cured must be alleviated . . . it is better that some hundred females of loose life should be entertained for a few hours in a single room, than that they should be encouraged to prowl about the street. Whatever thins the loose population of the Haymarket and Regent Street is so far a social gain. We ought to regard the interests, not of the profligate, but of the respectable. At all events, when vice is concentrated in Windmill Street, men must go in cold blood to seek it out, while flaunting on the *pave* it tempts the young and unwary. Few except extreme profligates would go to the recognised haunts of vice; but many fall under the public temptation of the streets who would avoid it in its own dancing and drinking saloons.

At any rate, the lesson taught by the change of opinion on the part of the Middlesex magistrates since last year is that it will not do to attempt the system of prosecuting these vicious places by instalments. There is already power in the common law to hunt down immorality by units and in detail. All immoral houses can be suppressed by the parochial authorities – all street walkers may be arrested by the police. But to carry out the law is simply impossible. What is cut down in one street grows up in the next . . . it is no use to prohibit – all that we can do is regulate . . . Let authority deal with any offence against public decency; let the magistrate, or the police, receive additional powers to repress public offences; but the failure of the attempt to put down the Argyll Rooms shows that we are beginning to understand that the control is better than an abortive attempt to prohibit.

By 1862 the *Saturday Review* was becoming more pointed in its views on street prostitution and the attempts of the anti-vice lobby to force government action to suppress it. The following article was unusually explicit in setting out its view of the nature of the problem and the shortcomings of the anti-vice lobby.

'The Haymarket', Saturday Review, 7 June 1862

On Saturday last, what is called an influential deputation . . . waited on the Home Secretary. The subject matter of their complaint was the nightly gaieties of which the upper part of the Haymarket and several neighbouring streets are the scene. It is indeed a striking sight – one which no foreigner who wishes to study our national morality in all its aspects ought to overlook. It is seen in all its glory on a fine summer's night at one o'clock . . . The pavement is occupied in force by crowds of men and women, who saunter about in the blaze of gaslight which issue from the aggregation of gin-palaces and oyster shops of which the street consists . . . Their conversation, it is needless to say, is frank and candid, expressing pointedly and unreservedly the subject matter of their meditations and the desires of their hearts. There is no room for any charitable self-delusion as to the character of this assemblage of men and women, or the nature of the deities in whose worship they are engaged. . . .

Many circumlocutions have undoubtedly been invented to describe . . . the highly tinted Venuses who form so favourite a study of the connoisseurs of the Haymarket. Some call them 'social evils', others . . . call them 'unfortunate women', others, who are more respectful . . . are satisfied to describe them as 'gay persons'. But, on the whole, the nicest, the softest, the most poetical designation we have heard is that which the Penitentiaries have invented – 'Soiled Doves' . . .

It is fair to the influential deputation to say that they were not restrained from stating their case in all its nudity by any fears of shocking the sensitive ears of Sir George Grey. . . . The soiled doves were becoming a formidable nuisance to the whole neighbourhood. Light sleepers could get no night's rest for their incessant cooings. Respectable women could not pass the streets for fear of being pecked at by them. Philanthropists who had taken the trouble to visit all their haunts . . . stated to Sir George Grey . . . that soiled doves were to be frequently found in the gin-shops of the Haymarket, and that their presence in the streets acted as a temptation to young men . . .

All these complaints were laid before the Home Secretary, and very

Midnight in the Haymarket, London, *c.* 1860. (Mayhew, *London.* Mary Evans Picture Library)

courteously received . . . but he could give the deputation little comfort. He could hold out hopes to them that, by putting the law more rigidly into executing, or sharpening its provisions, it might be possible to drive the soiled doves out of the gin-shops. . . . But such measures would only drive them in greater multitudes into the streets; and as the whole object of the deputation was to drive them out of the streets, the prospect held out was anything but satisfactory . . .

The Continental practice was frequently referred to, but only to draw from both sides the unanimous judgement that 'the state of public opinion in this country' will not allow it to be adopted here. It is obvious enough that the police cannot clear the streets unless they are allowed to remove the obstructions they are to remove. In other words, they must know the 'soiled doves' by sight. In Continental countries, measures are taken to enable them to possess this knowledge. The dovecote is duly catalogued and registered. The result is that in Paris, or Berlin, or Vienna, such a scandal as the English Haymarket is never to be seen. There, the streets are safe for peaceable citizens to pass through at any time . . .

The open and obvious evil, which must strike the eye of all who come up the Haymarket late at night, is not the only one that results from our sage attempts to destroy facts by shutting our eyes to them. The secret workings of a far greater evil are well known to medical men. We can but barely allude to the frightful social dangers which the *police sanitaire* of the Continent is intended to avert . . . It is impossible to follow this subject up. It will suggest itself to everyone thoughts which we dare not clothe in words. But we cannot exclude from our minds dangers and evils which affect those yet unborn, or listen with patience to the prudish platitudes which hinder our Government from taking common sense methods to arrest the progress of a plague. The difficulty lies wholly in the scruples of the religious world . . . The only obstacles to a sensible policy upon this subject at home are the religious ostriches who think they have extirpated an evil by hiding their heads and refusing to hear its name.

A year later, public opinion had shifted sufficiently to allow the *Saturday Review* to discuss openly the problem of venereal disease in the armed forces, which had been under discussion in Whitehall covertly since the end of the Crimean War. This article from the *Review* of 12 September 1863 clearly paralleled official thinking about the problems of maintaining fighting efficiency with a disease-ridden military.

'The Sin in Scarlet', Saturday Review, *12 September 1863*

Although diligent public discussion of any subject of grave social importance often fails to produce any large or immediate result, it assuredly never leaves the matter where it was before. . . . Five years ago, there was a great ripping up of the skirts of society, and a very appalling exposure of the filth concealed under an outward show of extreme purity. The 'Social Evil' was elaborately investigated . . . and then, amid much excited writing and highly coloured, purposeless description, all practical results were gradually lost sight of, until at length the subject, worn threadbare, gradually dropped out of notice. To all appearances, harm rather than good had ensued . . .

Yet one good effect of the discussion to which we have referred was the impression made on those who had previously opposed any interference with, or legislation about, the existing evil . . . The revelations about the awful extent and wide spreading ramifications of this social sin startled them into a modification of their opinions . . . they were finally so far terrified by the hard facts and plain figures submitted to them as to acknowledge that Somebody ought to do Something.

Hence we hear nothing more now-a-days of any foolish propositions about extinguishing prostitution; yet this was once the great cry of the people to whom we refer . . . We do not believe, after the revelations recently made, that any will be found so unwise and thoughtless as to oppose earnest attempts to check the evil. The mischief done to the State and the nation by diseases which arise from sexual vice is incalculable. It has been computed (chiefly from hospital statistics) that two hundred women are newly infected every day in London, who have no other means of obtaining food and shelter than by communicating the diseases thus contracted. But even more startling . . . are the results of a recent official investigation as to the extent of the evil in the army and navy. We gather from the returns of a committee appointed to report on this subject that these loathsome diseases are six times more prevalent among British than among French or Belgian soldiers – the numbers each year being 70 for France, against 442 for England, in every 1,000 men. Turning to previous army medical reports, we find that this frightful prevalence of disease cannot be explained away by temporary or local causes, although in certain regiments and on certain stations the numbers are still higher. In the Coldstream Guards, during a twelve-month period, (1858–59), the total number of cases amounted to 875 in a force of 1,600 men. In the year 1859, the ratio per 1,000 in the Royal Artillery was 571.4, and in the Military Train 580.3 . . .

As is the health condition of the soldiers, so also is that of the marines and sailors. There is the same enormous extent of disease contracted, disabling the men from active service whilst under treatment. The egregious folly of permitting things to remain as they are is well exemplified by the condition of the crew of the great fighting iron plated ship, the *Warrior*. This vessel was built at fabulous cost, and was filled with picked men. She was employed on the Home Station, and during a year the daily loss of service from the causes referred to averaged upwards of 22 men, not less than 220 cases being treated out of a force of 711 men. These figures need no comment.

We turn now to the consideration of what can practically be done to mitigate the rapidly extending evil we have described . . . here the recommendations of the Committee appointed to investigate the subject are expressed with a laudable reserve; for it is far better to do a little efficiently than to attempt prematurely sweeping measures. . . . It is evident that the chief difficulty is not how to manage the diseased soldier, but how to prevent the healthy soldier from becoming diseased . . . So far as concerns him personally, it is only necessary to devise the means, since he is a servant of the State, and must submit to whatever regulations are considered essential to keep him effective as a soldier. For this object, the provision of rational amusement and employment to relieve that intolerable tedium of barrack life which drives him to seek relief in dissipation – the enforcement of health inspection, with punishment for concealing disease . . . and the confinement to barracks until an absolute cure is effected, are suggestions which . . . might be easily carried out, and would undoubtedly be of considerable value . . .

But the real difficulty commences when the means by which the infected woman may be prevented from spreading disease come to be considered . . . The courses open to the Government to adopt have been . . . narrowed to two. One is the establishment of some system analogous to that which exists elsewhere, for the compulsory registration and periodical medical inspection of all prostitutes. The alternative course is to take cognizance only of existing cases of disease. It is proposed to establish at all garrison and sea port towns Lock Hospitals for women, where they may be received when suffering from specific diseases, and detained until no longer liable to communicate infection. . . . This is at least a practical way of dealing with the evil as it exists . . . The money so laid out would be repaid many times over – to view the question in no other light – by the saving which would be effected in our army expenditure.

The proposition to enforce some system of registering and periodically examining loose women presents a vast number of difficulties not thoroughly appreciated by those who draw their conclusions only from military experience. The Continental coercive system, as carried out in Belgium, has been found not only to diminish greatly the number of cases, but it is also reported that the more virulent forms of disease, such as shatter the constitutions of our soldiers, are now-a-days never met with at Brussels. It must be remembered, however, that there exists in Belgium a police supervision for protecting the civil as well as the military population from the evils which we have described; and it is just the want of this which stands in the way of any radical treatment of the subject as it affects our own troops . . .

We can form some opinion as to the efficiency of authoritative control in diminishing the evil under consideration, from certain official concerns recently received from Malta. In that island the *femmes publiques* have, since 1825, been subject to stringent police regulations . . . But in 1859 police inspections were pronounced illegal and discontinued . . . The spread of the disease was so rapid in the island that in June 1861, the system of inspection was revived. And in November 1862, the high authority [Deputy Inspector-General of Hospitals] . . . reports 'Up to this date not a single case has been contracted in this island. I beg to submit the results which have attended the re-establishment of the law, and which I believe should exist in all localities where large bodies of seamen and soldiers are congregated, as at our sea ports and garrisons.'

The subject of the health of our army and navy, as influenced by one particular form of disease, is of such vital importance that we have not shrunk from the task of putting it plainly before our readers. It is a most repulsive and painful topic, but the responsibility of dealing with it cannot be evaded. It is not easy to understand why we should continue to consider ourselves better than those of our neighbours who have long ago found it essential for public safety to control an evil which can never be entirely subjugated while human nature is what it is. It is only gross hypocrisy and pharasaical self conceit to pretend that we alone are exempt from the common curse, and are not as other men are.

7. The Contagious Diseases Acts

By 1864 the public health lobby outside parliament was increasingly confident that it could secure legalisation and regulation of female prostitution along Continental lines. Behind the prudish façade of mid-Victorian respectability, the official attitude was not only fully aware of the officially intolerable extent of commercial sex, but was moving toward legal toleration – at least where the military and naval other ranks were concerned. Public health lobbyists were well aware that their arguments were winning support in military circles around Whitehall. A long article which appeared in the *Lancet* on 19 March 1864 (pp. 327–9) examined the situation as seen from the public health perspective. It was commenting on the Whitbread report which had just investigated the impact of venereal diseases on the military. The fact that the report had been commissioned carried its own significance. The article summarised the evidence presented by commanding officers and military medical experts and discussed the conclusions of the report, which were at variance with its own support for state-regulated prostitution.

'Venereal Disease in the Army and Navy'

The enormous prevalence of venereal disease in the army and navy which the annual reports of the medical officers of those services disclose . . . have now for some years forcibly arrested the attention of the heads of departments . . . Year after year the detailed reports of the medical officers have displayed more clearly the frightful ravages which venereal diseases occasion . . . The Government, with the view of feeling their way towards some practicable method of meeting the evil, issued a commission more than twelve months since to inquire into the subject, and they made a 'confidential report' thereon . . . Lord Clarence Paget recently referred to the report which they have made as being of a character to demand the most serious attention of the government; . . . for the members of the medical profession these facts have a very general and deep interest . . .

They conclude that any system of medical inspection, if enforced against the wish of the women, would prove delusive. They recommend ample subscriptions to Lock Hospitals, and enlarged accommodation for diseased women. They call for the suppression of the brothel beer houses . . . They urge that greater facilities for washing in private are much required both in barracks and on board ship. With great wisdom they press upon the Government the necessity of providing the soldiers and sailors with all those means of healthy and rational occupation in industry and recreation which can keep them from the haunts of listlessness and vice. They recommend that regiments fresh from foreign stations and flush of money should not be quartered in stations notorious for venereal disease.

To all this Sir John Liddell* adds a rider, in which we heartily concur. The Committee, he says, have in these timid recommendations not touched the source of disease, and all that they advise will do little or nothing to arrest the mass of disease of which they speak as one as being appalling . . . Sir John Liddell has no more hope than we have that, if all the recommendations be carried out, any diminution of syphilis will be effected. It appears to him that the only sure means of mitigating the ravages of syphilis, and probably of causing its entire disappearance, is to superintend, by compulsory examination and cure, the health of the public women who propagate it.

All the army and navy reports from commanding and medical officers are in favour of this measure. Some few express doubts of its practicability . . . but none question its importance and value. As to the difficulty of reconciling the people of this country to such useful preventive measures, we very much doubt whether it is not greatly exaggerated. The people of England are, perhaps, the most ready in the world to adopt new customs and to alter their modes of thought on occasion . . . The introduction with general assent of that for compulsory vaccination, of house inspections by sanitary commissioners, of the visitation of butchers' shops, and the enforcement of penalties for selling diseased meat and so forth, are all precedents which show that the general welfare is admitted to be a sufficient guarantee for measures of inspection and prevention . . . If the butcher's shop may be occasionally visited and inspected for diseased meat, why should the brothel be exempted? . . . We have stringent provisions attached to the Health of Towns Act, and why should not these be included? It is a disease now far more fatal and general than smallpox, and scientifically not less within reach of preventive measures. Medical men do well, then, we are persuaded, repeatedly and energetically to call upon

* Sir John Liddell was Director General of the Medical Department of the Navy and gave evidence to the 1857–8 Commission into the Sanitary Conditions of the Army.

Government to arm science with the social powers necessary to destroy this spreading cancer of civilisation . . .

By the summer of 1864 the public health lobby was aware that this line of argument was in the ascendant in Whitehall. An entirely justified confidence is exhibited in the following report of a meeting of the Epidemiological Society. Significantly, the papers were introduced by medical officers from the navy and military, while the discussion was attended by William Acton. The report is taken from the *Lancet*, 16 June 1864, p. 705.

'The Prevention of Syphilis'

A highly interesting discussion on the prevention of syphilis took place at the last meeting of the Epidemiological Society. The subject was brought before the Society by Dr Dickson RN, in a paper on the prevention of syphilis in the navy; and by Dr Francis Brown, late of the Coldstream Guards, in a paper on the Prevalence of Enthetic Diseases amongst the troops serving in the United Kingdom. Dr Dickson illustrated the influence of police regulations in diminishing the amount of syphilis in the navy by an account of a serious outbreak . . . on board the *Chesapeke* . . . She carried fifty guns, and a crew of about 550 men. During the short campaign in the north of China in the summer of 1859 she had suffered much from sickness . . . When the campaign was over, . . . the crew, being much in need of relaxation, were permitted monthly to go ashore forty-eight hours. The men had just received the bounty voted them by Parliament, and . . . they were undoubtedly more than usually licentious. In the seven months the relaxation lasted no fewer than 195 of the crew contracted venereal disease, and were incapacitated for duty . . . Other ships in the harbour suffered similarly from the loathsome malady . . . Dr Dickson suggested to the naval commander in chief, Admiral Sir Jas. Hope, a mode of procedure . . . Hong Kong possesses a system of police in relation to prostitution. According to the laws of the colony, prostitutes to whom Europeans resort must be registered, and they must submit themselves to the colonial surgeon for inspection at stated intervals . . . These laws had fallen into disuse, but it was determined by the Admiral to seek their enforcement. When a man presented himself to the ship's surgeon suffering from venereal [sic], he was asked if he knew where and from whom he had obtained the malady, and if he could identify the person. If he could, he was sent with the master at arms to lodge a complaint before the magistrate. Upon this complaint, action was taken; and the end was that, whereas during the first part of the stay of the *Chesapeke* in harbour an average of forty applicants for treatment would follow each forty-eight hours leave on shore, in the latter part the number was reduced to eight or ten . . .

Dr Bowen laid before the Society an able summary of the losses suffered by the army on the home stations from venereal, and forcibly showed the necessity which existed, . . . Measures may be readily applied both as regards the army and the navy . . . The chief difficulty rests in suggesting measures of relief on the home stations which would not clash with the natural prejudices of the public. Dr Dickson thought . . . that police regulations might be devised, productive of much good in seaport towns, and which need not run counter to the prepossessions of the public. Dr Bowen entertained a like view in regard to the army. . . . They thought, moreover, that much good could be done in enlightening the public and facilitating the control of venereal if the Epidemiological Society would take up the question. In these views they were strongly supported by Staff-surgeon Crawford, MD, Dr Mackay, RN, and Mr Acton. Dr Mackay trusted that if the Society moved in the question it would not confine its attention solely to the army and navy. Mr Acton pointed out that the public must grow into the knowledge of this important subject. It was a disheartening subject to work upon, as it could not be obtruded both in season and out of season, as many sanitary questions; but it was a subject which peculiarly called for the aid of the learned societies . . . Mr Radcliffe undertook to submit the suggestions of Dr Dickson and Dr Bowen to the Council of the Society.

Events were, however, outstepping the careful deliberations of the experts. The government had by now been convinced by the arguments over the military cost of venereal disease, and was already drafting an Act which would set up an experimental system of regulating prostitution in garrison and naval towns with the effect of supplying disease-free women for the other ranks. This measure, which was bound to outrage both civil liberty and moral purity campaigners, was prepared with great secrecy and circulated only to interested parties in and around Whitehall. Among those who could not be ignored was Florence Nightingale, although she was both a liberal and a moral puritan. When shown the draft she was shocked, writing to Harriet Martineau on 31 May 1864 that 'I don't believe any Ho of C will pass this bill. Any honest girls might be locked up all night by mistake by it.' She was to be mistaken. Martineau was prompted to write a powerful article on 2 July 1864 for the *Daily News* which, although full of circumlocutions rendering it obscure to the general public, carried an unmistakable message to the well informed that the Bill should be rejected.

Daily News, *2 July 1864*

It is an awkward and difficult state of things when legislation is necessary, or is sought without being necessary, on matters unfit to be brought before the eye of a great part of the public. The awkwardness and difficulty, however, are no justification to journalists for permitting the slightest risk of bad legislation. The Bill brought in by Lord Clarence Paget, and called 'The Contagious Diseases Bill' is of this nature. If this Bill had a fair chance of careful examination by persons of an accurate habit of mind, it would be speedily prevented doing further mischief than the proposal of it has done already . . .

The fear is that such an examination is not likely to be obtained. The object of the proposer is to get the Bill passed with as little noise and as few words as possible . . . In the position of the mover it is very natural that he should do what he is doing – endeavour to obtain a committee so large that, when the Bill has passed it, the house will accept the matter without discussion, but a responsibility is thus thrown on the committee which no man of them all can take to heart too seriously . . . In plain words, here is a Bill which promises to secure soldiers and sailors from the consequences of illicit pleasures. It invariably happens that such protection creates a false security, however careful the legislature may be. This Bill is our first step into that province of legislation. It is a step which can never be so retracted as to leave us undamaged; while, if not retracted, it must lead us on to attempt a similar protection on behalf of civil society. Yet, all important as such an initiatory measure must be, the one before the House is full of ill defined or undefined terms, provisions for punishing unproved or unprovable offences, and for remedying evils which cannot be ascertained to exist. It is not conceivable that the House will pass such a Bill, if its members will but compel their attention to it. If it was framed by a faultless intelligence, it would be a fearful venture; but, vague, ineffective, and delusive as it is in its whole fabric, it passage would be a national calamity . . .

This article did not merely set out objections to the Act, but made a crucial claim which was to inflame the indignation of its opponents – the allegation that the Bill was being rushed through parliament by underhand means without the full import being discussed by MPs. The article fell initially on stony ground. While it set the terms for a struggle which would last for the next two decades, it failed to influence the government. At the behest of the Secretary of State for War, Earl de Grey, the Bill was introduced into the Commons late on 20 June 1864. It passed the Commons on 21 July, and went through the Lords in a mere six days. Royal Assent was given on 29 July. During a process which lasted little more than five weeks, not a single word of debate was uttered in either House. In this distinctly unsatisfactory manner, the government set up a system of state-regulated prostitution which dominated debate on prostitution for the next two decades.

The Contagious Diseases Act 1864, 27 and 28 Victoria, c. 85, Cap LXXXV

An Act for the Prevention of Contagious Diseases at Certain Naval and Military Stations, 29th July 1864
Whereas it is expedient to make Provisions calculated to prevent the spreading of certain Contagious Diseases in the Places to which this Act applies: Be it therefore enacted

1. This Act may be cited as the Contagious Diseases Prevention Act, 1864.

3. The Places to which this Act applies shall be the Places mentioned in the First Schedule* hereto, the Limits of which Places shall for the Purposes of this Act be such as are defined in that Schedule . . .

11. Where an Information, in the Form given in the Second Schedule to this Act, or to the like effect, is laid before a Justice of the Peace by a Superintendent or Inspector of Metropolitan Police, or by a Superintendent or Inspector of Police or Constabulary authorised to act in any Place to which this Act applies, or by any Medical Practitioner duly registered as such, the Justice may, if he thinks fit, issue to the woman named in the Information a Notice in the Form given in the same Schedule, or to the like effect.

12. A Constable or other Peace Officer shall serve such Notice on the Woman to whom it is directed, by delivering the same to her personally, or by leaving the same with some Person for her at her last or usual Place of Abode . . .

14. Such Order shall be a sufficient Warrant for any Constable or Peace Officer to whom the Order is delivered, to apprehend such Woman, and to convey her with all practicable speed to the Hospital thereby named . . . for the purpose of ascertaining whether she has a Contagious Disease, and in case, on such Examination, it is ascertained that she has a Contagious Disease, then to

---

* The First Schedule named eleven towns as being covered by the Act, namely Portsmouth, Plymouth, Woolwich, Chatham, Sheerness, Aldershot, Colchester, Shorncliffe, and, in Ireland, The Curragh, Cork, and Queenstown.

detain her in the Hospital for Twenty-four Hours from the Time of her being brought there . . .

16. Within the said period of Twenty-four Hours the Authorities of such Hospital shall cause a certificate, signed by the Medical Officer who has made such examination, stating (if the fact be so) that on such Examination it has been ascertained that such Woman has a Contagious Disease, to be made out and laid before the Justice by whom the order was made, or some other Justice having like jurisdiction; and thereupon such Justice may, if he thinks fit, order the Authorities of such Hospital to detain such Woman in the Hospital for Medical Treatment until discharged by such Authorities, and such Order shall be a sufficient warrant to such Authorities to detain such Woman, and such Authorities shall detain her accordingly; provided that no Woman shall be detained under any such Order for a longer Period than Three Months.

17. If any Woman ordered as aforesaid to be taken to a Certified Hospital for Medical Examination refuses to submit to such Examination, or if any Woman ordered to be detained in a Certified Hospital for Medical Treatment refuses or wilfully neglects while in the Hospital to conform to the Regulations thereof, or quits the Hospital without being discharged from the same as aforesaid, every such Woman shall be guilty of an Offence against this Act, and on summary Conviction thereof before Two or more Justices of the Peace shall be liable to Imprisonment in the Case of a First Offence, for any term not exceeding One Month and in the Case of a Second or any subsequent Offence for any Term not exceeding Two Months.

18. If any person, being the Owner or Occupier of any House, Room, or Place within the Limits of any Place to which this Act applies, or being a Manager or Assistant in the Management thereof, knowing or having reasonable Cause to believe any common Prostitute to have a Contagious Disease, induces or suffers such common Prostitute to resort to or be in such House, Room or Place for the Purpose of Prostitution, every such person shall be guilty of an Offence against this Act, and on summary Conviction thereof before Two or more Justices of the Peace shall be liable to a Penalty not exceeding Ten Pounds, or, at the discretion of the Justices, to be imprisoned for any Term not exceeding Three Months, with or without Hard Labour . . .

23. This Act shall continue in force for Three Years from the passing thereof, and no longer.

The 1864 Act was followed in 1866 by a second Act which made the system permanent, and a third Act in 1869 which extended the system although still confining it to towns of military and naval use. As the Contagious Diseases Acts slipped through parliament, however, the campaigners for the extension of the system to the civilian population grew more eloquent. The *British Medical Journal* provided a platform for this campaign which was less strident than the *Lancet*. A prominent supporter of the Extension campaign was Berkeley Hill, Surgeon to the Lock Hospital and Assistant Surgeon to University College Hospital. In this contribution to the *BMJ* of 23 May 1868 (pp. 505–6), Hill offers an admirably objective investigation of the state of prostitution in London, while using his findings skilfully to support the extension campaign.

'The Venereal Disease among Prostitutes in London'

While investigating the effect of the Contagious Diseases Act 1866 in those towns where it is in force . . . I also undertook . . . to gather by systematic visitations . . . some knowledge of the extent to which the public women of London are afflicted with contagious disease . . . also, whether it would be practicable to apply to them the regulations that control the common prostitutes of garrison towns . . .

The great majority of women to whom prostitution is the business of life live together in localities that are perfectly well known to the police. This peculiarity very much facilitates the supervision necessary for the purpose of examination and control. Nor is the number, so far as can be learned, of the prostitutes in London unmanageably great. Though it is difficult to form an exact estimate, there is good reason for supposing that all the prostitutes, both avowed and clandestine, do not exceed 15,000; and probably this is an overestimate, for only between 6,000 and 7,000 are known to the police.

But, passing to the question of disease among them, the result of my inquiries convinced me that very nearly all of them sooner or later suffer from venereal disease of one kind of another. The women admitted this themselves; and the greater number could tell me what means they had employed to cure their disease, when they had it. The poorer ones, of course, had recourse to the hospital or workhouse; the richer had paid medical men to attend them. They all, nevertheless, use means for cure very inefficiently, and simply seek to get rid of pain or discomfort, without assuring themselves that their malady is cured before they return to prostitution . . . Even the women with whom men of the highest classes in society associate are nearly as careless in this respect as the wretched outcast of the street . . .

The poorer women have to contend with many difficulties to procure treatment. Most of them are very ignorant of all parts of London, except that in which they reside, or to which they resort to solicit the other sex. For instance, in the Ratcliffe Highway I found several women who had never heard of the Lock Hospital or the Royal Free Hospital; and some were even ignorant of the London Hospital close to them.

A second impediment is caused by most hospitals admitting very few patients of this class. There are only about 150 beds in London to receive all the women who have venereal disease; and the workhouses only take them in when they are wholly incapable from illness to make exertion of any kind . . . Should they apply for relief as outpatients, they have no convenience where they dwell for carrying out the directions of the surgeon. In the low lodging houses of Drury Lane, they live day by day in an underground kitchen, common to all the inmates of the house; and they have no access to the sleeping rooms until a fixed hour at night; water is scanty, and soap and towels are costly . . . Perhaps the best way of demonstrating the state of the women is to narrate a part of what I saw and heard when visiting the several low districts of London . . .

On my visit to Drury Lane, I entered a street in which, I was told, 300 thieves and prostitutes live . . . The first house I entered was a common lodging-house, and contained seventeen prostitutes . . . Nine women were sitting round the room for warmth; most doing nothing, one or two sewing; one, very drunk, was talking in a loud voice, and munching a crust. I first interrogated the deputy. She said that the women were very reckless; and though they always concealed their disease as long as possible, sooner or later she found it out, and then they were sent off. When turned out, they usually applied for admission at the Royal Free Hospital . . . otherwise they continued their prostitution, and attended as outpatients till they either recovered, or were admitted. When asked if the girls ever refrained from walking the streets while diseased, she said ''Tain't likely; if they did, they must starve.' . . .

In a court off Grays Inn Lane, we visited four houses entirely occupied by prostitutes. In one of them, we found in a small room, two girls of 20 and 21 years old . . . The first told me that up to a year and a half ago she worked at the mantle trade; but their work became scarce and she eked out her living with prostitution. Last winter she caught the disease . . . She remained in the Royal Free Hospital three months, in which time she had a sore throat and tongue, spots on the skin, and scabs in her hair. Since leaving the Royal Free Hospital, she had attended the Lock Hospital as an out-patient, but continued her prostitution at the same time. In answer to my queries respecting her willingness to submit to sanitary regulations, she replied she should not object to being examined by a doctor as often as was necessary . . . Her companion was equally ready to submit to the compulsory medical examination and detention, as were, indeed, all the women in these courts. Similar replies rewarded our inquiries in the courts and alleys between Grays Inn Road and Golden Lane . . .

Assistance is denied many through their being diseased, for the houses of most of the [Reclamation] societies have no accommodation for such persons, and accordingly they are rejected. At the Magdalene Hospital (where applicants are at once cautioned that they cannot be admitted if they are diseased) in 1866, 284 women were examined previously to being sent before the committee; forty-five were rejected for being diseased, and of 131 admitted in an apparently healthy state, fourteen afterward showed signs of syphilis. Again, out of 1,050 women who applied in one year to the Rescue Society for admission, 314 were or had previously been diseased . . .

The necessity for enforcing stringent sanitary regulations among the prosperous women of the town is no less evident, and there is good reason to believe that they also, like their destitute sisters, would raise but little opposition to examination and detention when diseased. These persons are very nearly as ignorant of the signs of disease as the others, and are often, through their reckless habits, quite unprovided, if their means of obtaining income are checked. They are also constantly exposing themselves to contagion without heed or precaution . . .

The most eloquent propagandist for the creation and extension of the Regulatory system was the doctor and writer William Acton. His book *Prostitution*, first published in 1857, was a major study and, coupled with a remarkable facility for publicity on the part of its author, played a significant role in raising the level of public awareness about the debate on prostitution. Acton's rational and well researched approach to the subject, particularly in his contributions to the medical press, undoubtedly played a considerable role in creating the climate of opinion in which the CD Acts were passed. However, not content with the limited regulation provided by the three CD Acts, Acton campaigned for their extension to the civilian population. These extracts are taken from the 1870 edition of the book, and illustrate the thrust of his argument. Acton's book is well known but often misinterpreted. These brief extracts demonstrate that it is not accurate to suppose that Acton believed in the figure of 80,000 prostitutes in London.

pp. 32–6
To obviate the possibility of misapprehension, I remind the reader that I regard prostitution as an inevitable attendant upon civilised, and especially close packed, population. When all is said and done, it is, and I believe ever will be, ineradicable. Whether its ravages, like those of disease and crime, may not be

modified by unceasing watchfulness – whether it may not be the duty of the executive, as a French writer suggests, to treat it as they do such ordinary nuisances as drains, sewers and so forth . . . it will be my business to inquire in a future chapter. In the present I shall offer as complete a survey of that portion of it which stalks abroad, *tête levée* ['with head erect'], in this metropolis,and other parts of the kingdom, as the facts at any English writer's disposal admit of.

The number of prostitutes in London has been variously estimated, according to the opportunities, credulity or religious fervour of observers . . . To attempt to reconcile or construct tables upon the estimates I have met with would be a hopeless task. I can merely give a few of the more moderate that have been handed down by my predecessors. Mr Colquhoun, a magistrate at the Thames Police Court, rated them at 50,000 some sixty years ago. The Bishop of Exeter spoke of them as reaching 80,000. Mr Talbot, secretary of a society for the protection of young females, made the same estimate. The returns on the constabulary force presented to parliament in 1839, furnished an estimate of 6,371 – viz., 3,732 'known to the police as kept by the proprietors of brothels', and 2,639 as resident in lodgings of their own, and dependent on prostitution alone for a livelihood. It was estimated by the Home authorities in 1841, that the corresponding total was 9,409 – which, I need hardly point out, does not include the vast numbers who regularly or occasionally abandon themselves, but in a less open manner.

I am indebted to the courtesy [sic] of Sir Richard Mayne, the late Chief Commissioner of the Metropolitan Police, for the subjoined return . . . [reproduced opposite]

The police have not attempted to include – in fact, could not have justly included, I must almost say – the unnumbered prostitutes whose appearance in the streets as such never takes place; who are not seen abroad at unseemly hours; who are reserved in manners, quiet and unobtrusive in their houses or lodgings, and whose general conduct is such that the most vigilant of constables could have no pretence for claiming to be officially aware of their existence or pursuits. The 1869 Report on the Contagious Diseases Act enables us for the first time to show the proportions of common prostitutes to soldiers at Aldershot. Thus, Inspector Smith gave in a report proving that there were, in June 1869, 243 recognised prostitutes to about 12,000 troops. This paucity of prostitutes, according to Dr Barr, causes some of them to have intercourse with 20 or 23 men in one night. (Report from the Select Committee on the Contagious Diseases Act, 1866, 1869, q. 751) . . .

I may here call attention to a lesson taught us pretty clearly by these returns, which is, that to attempt to put down prostitution by law is to attempt the impossible. Notwithstanding the numerous prosecutions and parish raids which have been directed against prostitutes and their dwellings during the past few years,

A Return of the number of Brothels and Prostitutes within the Metropolitan Police District, as nearly as could be ascertained at that date (May 20th, 1857).

Division	Number of Brothels					Number of Prostitutes			
	Where prostitutes are kept	Where prostitutes lodge	Where prostitutes resort	Total	Total returned in 1841	Well dressed, living in brothels	Well dressed, walking the streets	Low, infesting low neighbourhoods	Total
A	—	—	—	—	—	—	—	—	—
B	—	135	18	153	181	16	144	364	524
C	14	92	46	152	83	168	150	—	318
D	10	113	16	139	93	49	188	289	526
E	30	110	54	194	266	74	85	387	546
F	26	—	19	45	181	60	120	300	480
G	3	77	27	152	360	26	165	158	349
H	209	217	45	471	289	132	420	1251	1803
K	—	402	17	419	882	13	435	517	965
L	—	184	193	377	275	108	329	365	802
M	12	138	28	178	178	13	71	583	667
N	53	98	34	185	152	87	142	216	445
P	3	33	29	65	56	63	67	98	228
R	46	66	36	148	122	69	116	216	401
S	—	52	36	88	96	8	90	133	231
T	—	12	—	12	107	—	12	94	106
V	4	37	6	47	4	35	82	92	209
Total	410	1766	649	2825	3325	921	2616	5063	8600
Do. 1841	933	1544	848	3325	—	2071	1994	5344	9409

A. Whitehall, the Parks, Palaces, Government Offices.
B. Westminster, Brompton, Pimlico, part of Chelsea.
C. St James's, Regent-street, Soho, Leicester-square.
D. Marylebone, Paddington, St John's Wood.
E. Between Oxford-street, Portland-place, New-road, and Gray's-inn-lane.
F. Covent Garden, Drury-lane, St Giles's.
G. Clerkenwell, Pentonville, City-road, Shoreditch.
H. Spitalfields, Houndsditch, Whitechapel, Ratcliff.
K. Bethnal-green, Mile-end, and from Shadwell to Blackwall.

L. Lambeth and Blackfriars, including Waterloo-road, &c.
M. Southwark, Bermondsey, Rotherhithe.
N. Islington, Hackney, Homerton, &c.
P. Camberwell, Walworth, part of Peckham.
R. Deptford, Greenwich, and neighbourhood.
S. Kilburn, Portland, Kentish and Camden Towns to Cattle Market.
T. Kensington, Hammersmith, North End, Fulham.
V. Walham-green, Fulham, Chelsea, Cremorne.

Evidence from William Acton, *Prostitution*, 1857.

there were in the year 1868 1,756 houses where prostitutes lodge, against 1,766 in 1857. What can show more strongly the impossibility of (suppressing prostitution by the arm of the law)? [sic] Eleven years ago I pointed out that if a prostitute is prosecuted for plying her trade in one parish, she will only move into another. The result has proved the truth of my prediction, and recent failures add their testimony to that of world wide experience, and prove the impolicy of making attempts of this nature, except in cases when the houses proceeded against are shown to be productive of open scandal or a cause of intolerable nuisance.

I must observe that these returns give but a faint idea of the grand total of prostitution by which we are oppressed, as the police include in them only those women and houses whose nature is well and accurately known to them. There can be little doubt that numbers of women who live by prostitution lead apparently respectable lives in the lodgings or houses which they occupy; but all such are necessarily excluded from the returns.

Were there any possibility of reckoning all those in London who would come within the definition of prostitutes, I am inclined to think that the estimates of the boldest who have preceded me would be thrown into the shade . . .

Acton urged the adoption of the Continental system of state-regulated prostitution, to which end the CD Acts were a limited advance. In the following crucial section, he outlines the case for state regulation with a clarity unequalled by any other writer in the nineteenth century.

Acton on Prostitution, cont.

The question then arises, what is to be done with this system, at once injurious, imperishable, utterly sinful and abominable? There are, as we have seen, two methods of dealing with it, diametrically opposed to each other, in vogue in the civilised world. The one is adopted on the Continent, the other is adopted in England, and also in the United States. The former is the licensing, the latter the voluntary. They are of course based on entirely opposite principles. The LICENSING SYSTEM takes for its basis the indestructible nature of the evil and the terrible mischiefs which arise both socially and physically . . . it is argued that it is better . . . to regulate it . . . and to define the conditions subject to which it shall exist. The VOLUNTARY SYSTEM is based on the proposition that prostitution exists in defiance of the laws of God, that the only recognition which the state may lawfully take of sin is to suppress it, and that if this is inexpedient or impossible, the only alternative is to leave it to itself to find its own level and its own remedy . . . It is objected to the licensing system, that it is in fact licensing sin, and that in permitting indulgence under certain restrictions is in truth lending the sanction of the law to evil practices. It is also objected that it is practically useless, as the large majority of prostitutes contrive to evade its provisions. . . . even if it be taken as an objection against the system, it seems to be one of little weight, because the facts are clear that several thousand women are thereby rendered physically harmless . . . Surely the refusal to reap a considerable amount of benefit because we cannot reap all the benefit we desire is not wise. We should always bear in mind that half a loaf is better than no bread . . .

What is really meant is that the benefits derived from the licensing system are insignificant when compared with the evils introduced by it. The licensing system legalises vice by distinctly permitting it under certain given conditions, the result of which is to lend to prostitution the appearance, at least, of a lawful calling, and to diminish sensibly both in men and women the sense of shame. Such a lowering of the public morals is too dear a price to pay for partial security to the public health. Another argument is that it is degrading to the woman to be forced to publicly admit herself a harlot . . .

It is a somewhat curious style of arguing, to tell us in one breath that the system is bad, because it takes away from the shame naturally attaching to the life of a prostitute, and in the next that it is bad because it increases her degradation, and takes away, if submitted to, the last remnant of self respect . . . If the calling shall have ceased, by the operation of the law, to be a shameful one, there is no degradation in admitting publicly connection with it; if there is degradation in making this announcement, then the trade has not ceased to be shameful. These propositions cannot both be true at once; objectors to the licensing system must choose between them, and probably if they take their stand upon the first, their position will prove impregnable . . .

Whatever may be the failings of the licensing system, the demerits of the voluntary system seem not inconsiderable. This latter is a systematic refusal to admit certain facts and their consequences, whose existence no sane person would attempt to dispute, or even casual spectators fail to observe . . . the result is that disease carries on its ravages unchecked, private charity being unequal to the task of combating an enemy so gigantic. Our streets are a standing disgrace, the police being unable, with the limited authority intrusted to them, to cope with the disorderly characters that throng them . . .

It is difficult to choose between two evils, but happily for us the question is asked, and should be fairly answered, is there not some middle path that may be safely followed? The Contagious Diseases Act exhibits an attempt to steer between these two extremes. It may be that some of its provisions are open to criticism; but critics should not confound two systems utterly different in principle. Though to a certain extent analogous in their working, both involve the recognition of prostitution . . . The one, however, licenses the plying of a shameful trade on certain conditions fixed by law – in fact, legalises the system. The other proceeds on the theory that it is useless to deny or ignore the fact that prostitution exists, and that worse evils even than those which now oppress us might be apprehended from any attempts to repress it . . . but that at the same time, that it is a thing to be kept within certain bounds, and subjected to certain restraints and surveillence . . . Some assailants of the Contagious Act [sic] seem to confound it with the licensing system . . . I hope that I have said sufficient to show how entirely different the two methods really are. We must not confound recognition with license; to license prostitution is to license sin, and in a measure to countenance it. Recognition is not license, and has neither the appearance nor the effect of encouraging vice . . .

Recognition is the first step necessary to be made by those who would oppose any effectual barrier to the advance of prostitution. In vain do we build Lock Hospitals and penitentiaries to heal or reform those who by accident, as it were, have fallen into sin and reaped its bitter fruits . . . To what good general end do we rescue a few of these poor sufferers from time to time . . . leaving the multitudes to perish, . . . leaving the morass untouched, to extend as it pleases, and engulph all it can? To leave an open stinking ditch unclosed is bad enough – to leave the morass untouched is fatal . . . What we have to do is to close the approaches of this deadly swamp – to drain it, and to fill it up, and at the same time to disinfect its foul malarial streams, and prevent them flowing into purer soil . . . To do all this, we must take its measure, probe its depths, and accurately experience and understand its nature . . . What is this but recognition? The public are, I am happy to believe, at length awakening to a consciousness of the truth of this position, and the principle has received by the passing of the Contagious Diseases Act the sanction of the legislature, so that accomplished facts have to a certain extent closed the mouths of religious objectors . . . .

If Acton genuinely believed that the passing of the Contagious Diseases Act – presumably he means the third Act of 1869 – had closed the mouths of religious objectors, he was sadly mistaken. The next decade and a half would see a puritan Christian backlash which would not only destroy the Acts and the system they had erected, but resolve the debate over the legalisation or repression of prostitution decisively in favour of repression. Victorian values would become fixed in a most oppressive form and be stamped emphatically on British society.

8. The Emergence of the Puritan Reaction

The passing of the Contagious Diseases Acts had little impact on public opinion in their early years. Puritans, however, were steadily goaded into their most serious and sustained political intervention of the nineteenth century. In this they were aided by the creation of the first effective feminist agitation in British history. The most striking aspect of the campaign against the CD acts was the emergence of a separate women's section – the first time in British politics that women had set up an exclusively female political organisation. Its manifesto was the statement of the Ladies National Association, published on New Year's Day 1870. The 'famous Women's Protest', as Josephine Butler referred to it in her autobiography (*Personal Reminiscences of a Great Crusade*, 1896 edition, p. 17), set out the case as follows.

'The Women's Manifesto', as published in the Daily News, *1 January 1870*

We, the undersigned, enter our solemn protest against these Acts.

1st, because involving as they do such a momentous change in the legal safeguards hitherto enjoyed by women in common with men, they have been passed, not only without the knowledge of the country, but unbeknown, in a great measure, to Parliament itself; and we hold that neither the Representatives of the People, nor the Press, fulfil the duties which are expected of them, when they allow such legislation to take place without the fullest discussion.

2nd. Because, so far as women are concerned, they remove every guarantee of personal security which the law has established and held sacred, and put their reputation, their freedom, and their persons absolutely in the power of the police.

3rd. Because the law is bound, in any country professing to give civil liberty to its subjects, to define clearly an offence which it punishes.

4th. Because it is unjust to punish the sex who are the victims of vice, and leave unpunished the sex who are the main cause, both of the vice and its dreaded consequence; and we consider that liability to arrest, forced medical treatment, and (where this is resisted) imprisonment with hard labour, to which these Acts subject women, are punishments of the most degrading kind.

5th. Because by such a system, the path of evil is made more easy to our sons, and to the whole of the youth of England; inasmuch as a moral restraint is withdrawn the moment the state recognises, and provides convenience for, the practice of a vice which it thereby declares to be necessary and venial.

6th. Because these measures are cruel to the women who come under their action – violating the feelings of those whose sense of shame is not wholly lost, and further brutalising even the most abandoned.

7th. Because the disease which these Acts seek to remove has never been removed by any such legislation. The advocates of the system have utterly failed to show, by statistics or otherwise, that these regulations have in any case,

Glasgow police find that a respectable seeming private house is really a cover for a brothel.
(*The Day's Doings*, vol. 2, 3 June 1871, p. 312. Mary Evans Picture Library)

after several years trial, and when applied to one sex only, diminished disease, reclaimed the fallen, or improved the general morality of the country. We have, on the contrary, the strongest evidence to show that in Paris and other Continental cities where women have long been outraged by this system, the public health and morals are worse than at home.

8th. Because the conditions of this disease, in the first instance, are moral, not physical. The moral evil through which the disease makes its way separates the case entirely from that of the plague, or other scourges, which have been placed under police control or sanitary care. We hold that we are bound, before rushing into experiments of legalising a revolting vice, to try to deal with the *causes* of the evil, and we dare to believe that with wiser teaching and more capable legislation, those causes would not be beyond control.

The publication of the Women's Protest was an overnight sensation. Josephine Butler claimed that 'among the two thousand signatures which it obtained in a short time there were those of Florence Nightingale, Harriet Martineau, Mary Carpenter, the sisters and other relatives of the late Mr John Bright, all the leading ladies of the Society of Friends, and many well known in the literary and philanthropic world'. Butler later quoted an unnamed MP as having said to her 'We know how to manage any other opposition in the House or in the country, but this is very awkward for us – this revolt of women. It is quite a new thing; what are we to do with such an opposition as this?' (Butler, *Personal Reminiscences*, p. 20). The method adopted was simply to erect a wall of silence around the campaign. After the initial shock, the respectable press simply ignored it. The 'Repealers' were not deterred and quickly established a pressure group with branches in all major cities. It had a powerful appeal to trade unionists, whose members saw police power as a particular threat to working class wives and daughters. Josephine Butler had an especial sympathy with this section of society. She rapidly found herself the most charismatic speaker of the campaign, adopting an exhausting schedule of meetings – she spoke at ninety-nine in the first year alone. The National Association set up a regular publication, *The Shield*. The first edition was published on 7 March 1870, and the pages of the journal chart the movement's attempts to pursue both a parliamentary and an extra-parliamentary strategy in tandem. There was constant tension between these two elements of the campaign, but in the opening months both were used effectively. The leader of the parliamentary group was the Liberal Quaker MP Henry Fowler.

Henry Fowler opened the parliamentary offensive against the Contagious Diseases Act on 25 May 1870 with a motion for the Repeal of the Acts. The government did not

Josephine Butler. (Mary Evans/Fawcett Library)

take up a position for or against the Acts, and the Home Secretary H.A. Bruce cut the heart from the discussion by a brief announcement that 'The Government were prepared to authorize the issue of a Royal Commission'. He gave no reasons for this decision, but both sides had to accept this with confident assertions that the Commission would support their position. The following day *The Times* carried a leader vigorously supporting the Acts in the terms which expressed the anti-Repeal case.

The Times, *25 May 1870*

. . . We have done our best to keep clear of a discussion which is by no means inviting, but now that the agitation has come to the point of presenting a Bill for the repeal of an Act which was only brought into complete form last year, and which consequently has had only a few months' trial, we are compelled to face the subject, and protest against any such reversal of legislation.

Any utilitarian reasoning will probably seem cold-blooded and profane to people who have lashed themselves into such a state of moral sensibility as the opponents of the new law . . . The speakers appeal to what they imagine to be lofty considerations, and indeed, their point of view is so high that it is difficult to get up to it . . . Still more perceptible is the female influence which gives the movement novelty and vivacity, and consequently, to some extent, success . . . A thousand voices have repeated for the last six months that in endeavouring to check certain diseases we are impiously striving to take the rod out of the hand of God, and that in relieving the most wretched and degraded class of sufferers we are crushing the seeds of self respect which might otherwise spring up and blossom into fairer and holier nature. But when a man has listened to all this . . . he is compelled . . . to return to the very unpleasant facts of the case, . . . and into the provisions of the Acts themselves . . .

. . . In an able and comprehensive speech Dr [Lyon] Playfair took a review of the whole subject, refuting the arguments of Mr Fowler . . . showing the necessity for the Acts . . . The state of the Army was such that the daily loss to the service was equal to that of two regiments, and in the Navy it was computed that in a single year 7,000 men were more or less affected . . . The first point of the case then may be taken as proved, and in face of the evidence from all sides we cannot conceive how anyone can doubt that the second is proved also – namely, that the new law does diminish the disease. . . .

These arguments were vehemently disputed by the Repealers, and it was now clear that the silence of the 1860s was over. The Contagious Diseases Acts were now a matter of public controversy. And while the Royal Commission creaked into action, the point was reinforced by a notable by-election in the autumn of 1870.

The Repealers' extra-parliamentary strategy in 1870 focused on the attempts of Gladstone's first government to find a seat for Sir Henry Storks, a military man who was a strong supporter of the CD Acts. The events which followed are described by Repealer Benjamin Scott in his unofficial history of the Repeal movement, *A State Iniquity* (1890), pp. 124–8.

'The Colchester By-Election, 3 November 1870'

The Government was a Liberal one, headed by Mr W.E. Gladstone. It was incredible to the Government and the party managers that the Repealers, who were almost all at that time of the same party, would venture to strike at its supremacy. But the time was at hand when the party leaders would understand that a new force had come into the political arena . . .

It chanced at this time that the Government wanted an army organizer, as Under Secretary to the War Minister, . . . who was then making great changes in the army . . . They selected Sir Henry Storks, the ex-Governor of Malta, a great enthusiast for the Acts, who had enforced them with ruthless severity in the island . . .

It was impossible for the Repealers to accept such a person. His selection was the clearest evidence that the Government cared nothing for the agitation. The government knew that he was the *bête noir* of Repealers, for he had stood for Newark when Dr Bell Taylor and Mr Worth, of Nottingham, had followed him all over the town haranguing the people and distributing bills, until he withdrew his candidature. There occurred a vacancy at Colchester, a place under the Acts, and the Government determined to bring Storks into the House of Commons for the place. This put the Repealers on their mettle . . .

It was rightly considered the best strategy to draw off some of the Liberal electors from Storks and let the Conservative in, although he was unfriendly to repeal. Dr Baxter Langley, then a member of the National Association . . . was chosen as its champion . . .

Mrs Butler and Professor Stuart, with others, went down to Colchester to join the fray. Their campaign was commenced by the holding of earnest prayer meetings, whereat they gained strength and courage. Then they went into the streets. They distributed thousands of handbills containing Sir Henry Storks' views on prostitution, and a statement made by him to the House of Commons Committee that 'Not only prostitutes, but also SOLDIERS WIVES OUGHT TO BE EXAMINED!'

The blood of the Liberal partisans was up. They attacked the hotel in which Mrs Butler and her friends were staying, and when Dr Baxter Langley began to hold meetings they went mad and created a riot . . . Dr Langley tried to hold a meeting in the theatre, but he and Professor Stuart were . . . driven from the platform and chased to their hotel, which they reached, Langley covered with flour and dirt from head to foot, his clothes torn, his face bleeding, and Stuart wounded in the arm by a heavy blow . . . The followers of Storks may have justified this playfulness as one of the amenities of political warfare, but there was no sort of justification for the next thing they did. They posted on the walls an exact description of Mrs Butler's dress in order that she might be recognized and mobbed . . . Her friends never addressed her by her name in the street lest some listener should rally the ever present mob to attack her . . . On one occasion, after repeated flights from different houses, a room was taken for her in a Tory hotel, under the name of Grey. There she had gone to bed, and was falling asleep when she heard a knock on the door of her room, followed by the shout of the proprietor, 'Madam, I am sorry to find you are Mrs Butler; please get up and dress at once and leave the house. The mob are round the house, breaking the windows. They theaten to set fire to it if you don't leave at once . . .' Then he harangued the mob whilst Mrs Butler was dressing, and, led by one of the servant girls, ran along a little back street as fast as she could go, until she found shelter . . .

The violence of passion was not limited to the street mob. A Wesleyan minister in the town wrote a letter against Storks, and for thus daring to express a righteous opinion not held by his infuriated flock, these pious folk drove him from his church and the town . . .

The circumstances of the contest had attracted attention from all parts of the kingdom. . . . The result was going to be a serious blow to either the Government or the Repealers. The latter were exultant. Their courage and the brutal cruelty of the Liberals had brought about a reaction in their favour . . . At the general election of 1868 the voting was,

Liberal	1,467
Conservative	1,284
Majority	183

But at this election in 1870 the voting was,

Learmouth (Conservative)	1,396
Storks (Liberal)	869
Conservative Majority	527

It was a great victory for the Repealers. The Government were mortified. They saw they had to reckon with this new party. They must save themselves by silencing these powerful speakers. They did so by immediately announcing the grant of a ROYAL COMMISSION to consider the whole question. It was a shrewd method of paralysing the action of the repealers and yet keeping on foot the system they abhorred.

Scott was carried away by emotion. The Royal Commission had been announced nearly six months earlier and had nothing to do with the by-election. Gladstone's government did not regard the Repeal Campaign as significant, rightly judging it to be of marginal interest. Scott displays an over-estimation of the importance of Repeal which was widely shared among Repealers. *The Times* report of 4 November barely mentions Repeal as a factor in the by-election. In Colchester itself, the impact of the Repeal was greater than *The Times* acknowledged, but in the wider perspective its estimation was accurate.

The moral purity campaign did, however, have sufficient support to force Gladstone's government not only grant a Royal Commission, but to ensure that it represented both sides of the argument. However, this meant that the eventual report, issued in July 1871, was ruined. It attempted to satisfy both sides of an irreconcilable divide by an unworkable compromise. The system was to be maintained but the most controversial aspect of it – the compulsory examination of prostitutes – would be curtailed. The Commission declined to extend the system to the civilian population. This attempt at compromise between the advocates of extension and the advocates of repeal failed. Although all twenty-three members signed the report, there were seven signed notes of dissent. Sixteen of the commissioners dissented from some aspect of the report, seven being convinced extensionists and six being convinced repealers. The commission was so badly divided that the report satisfied no one.

The sections extracted here deal with the attempted compromise. An extract from Josephine Butler's evidence is also given. Intransigent and high handed though it was – and it was undoubtedly far less effective than the arguments of civil libertarians like John Stuart Mill – this sets out the arguments of the most dedicated campaigner against the CD Laws at their most characteristic.

Recommendations of the Royal Commission on the
Contagious Diseases Acts, 1871

48. The principal objection is to the periodical examination, which all the

medical witnesses engaged in the administration of the Acts concur in representing as essential to their efficiency. We are satisfied from their evidence that the frequent examination of women is the most efficacious means of controlling the disease, although a marked diminution was attained before recourse was had to this system. But even granting that the regular attendance before a surgeon is a vital part of the system, it becomes a grave question whether the system could be maintained in the face of objections, which, on moral grounds, have been raised against it . . . It is difficult . . . to escape from the inference that the state, in making provision for alleviating its evils, has assumed that prostitution is a necessity. There is some evidence that the women themselves consider that they are a privileged class; some of them are called 'Queen's women'; . . . there is also some slight evidence that the protected districts are resorted to by strangers for the purpose of safe indulgence . . . But whatever may be the moral effect of the periodical examination on the public women, we are assured that a large proportion, if not a majority of them, appreciate the benefit of a vigilant watch over their health, and that the regular attendance at the examination room has wrought an improvement in their demeanour, dress and general condition . . .

49. We have come to the conclusion, however, that though the periodical examination of common prostitutes is the most effectual mode of dealing with venereal disease, it would be difficult if not practically impossible to make the system general, even if on other grounds it would be desirable to do so. Thus, while the disease is general throughout the country the remedy for it would be confined to a few favoured places; a state of things which we likewise believe could not be permanently maintained.

50. We are therefore brought to the question, whether these Acts shall be repealed, or whether some modification of them may not be recommended by which they might be stripped of their anomalous and offensive character without materially impairing their efficiency.

51. We think that such modification may be arrived at. Notwithstanding the summary period which was put to the Act of 1864, there is evidence . . . that if allowed fair play it could work with vigour and efficiency . . .

53. . . . . The periodical examination of prostitutes being abolished, we would return to the proceedings taken under the Act of 1864, which dealt directly with the disease. We would continue in existence the certified hospitals already

established . . . In the event of prostitutes entering the hospitals voluntarily, we think that the authorities should have the power of retaining the patients until cured. The Acts of 1866 and 1869, with the exception of the sections relating to periodical examination . . . should continue in force within the prescribed limits, and at any military camps which may be temporarily formed, as measures of sanitary police applicable to the army and navy . . .

Josephine Butler's Evidence to the Royal Commission,

18 March 1871

12,869. You have stated that you entertain an objection to these Acts upon principle. Would you have the kindness to explain that a little more?

In the original protest issued by the Ladies National Association in January 1870 there occur the following words which express very well my own sense of the matter: 'We protest against this legislation, inasmuch as a moral restraint is withdrawn the moment the State recognises and provides convenience for a vice, which by providing this convenience it declares to be necessary and venial.' The expression used is – a moral restraint. . . . We claim that laws shall not be made which teach, in an indirect and subtle, but most effectual manner, that impurity of life is not a sin but a necessity. . . . Neither can our moral objections to these Acts be met by assurances that a certain number of women are reclaimed under their operations. I ask where are the men reclaimed by them? As mothers of sons we demand to know what the influence of these Acts is on young men. It is vain to restore fallen women to virtue on the one hand, while on the other you stimulate the demand for these victims. Prove to us, if you can, that these Acts promote chastity among men, for that is what we are concerned about.

12,870. I gather from that passage, which is your own, I presume?

It is my own.

12,871. That you consider a law which requires women who are gaining their livelihood by prostitution to submit to a periodical examination in order to guard against their communicating a loathsome disease, is a withdrawal of moral restraint?

It is a regulating of vice for the facilitating of its practice. It is a lowering of the moral standard in the eyes of the people . . .

12,872. You think that the construction that people put on these Acts is, that prostitution is in some senses legalised?

Not only think so, but know it to be the fact, in Scotland and the whole of the north of England . . .

12,873. And you concur in that opinion?

Entirely . . .

12,875. Then there would be no alteration of these Acts which could possibly reconcile them to you?

None whatever.

12,876. You would be satisfied with nothing but their entire repeal?

Nothing but their entire repeal . . .

12,877. Then supposing these Acts were repealed, you could suggest no mode by which the State could interfere and regulate or check this evil?

Not to regulate, but we have abundant suggestions by which the State may check profligacy, not with the object of curing disease only, but to check the vice which is the cause of the disease.

12,878. Would you favour the Commission with one?

We have them drawn up in form, but it would be premature to lay them before the Commission just now. No doubt it will all come before you in due time; at present I will only give you a general idea of what we have to suggest, both in the way of legislative enactments and other ways, reminding you that the great evil, with its unpleasant physical consequences, must be met from a variety of sides at once. Legislation alone will not do it. Seduction must be punished. At present for the purposes of seduction only, our law declares every female child a woman at 12 years of age. I am ashamed to have to confess to such a shameful state of the law before you gentlemen, but a child is a woman, for that purpose alone, at 12 years of age . . . The law of bastardy must be altered. At present the responsibility of illegitimate children is thrown on the mothers only, the fathers are irresponsible. Better laws in this direction would aid in diminishing the causes of prostitution. A higher standard of public opinion as to the vice of men – that is a thing in which we women are most deeply interested . . . above all things a higher standard with regard to the morality of men is needed and we, thousands of us, are banded together to attain that if possible . . . with your permission, I will just call your attention to this, that whereas all legislation hitherto which is at all of the right kind [sic] has been directed against one sex only, we insist that it shall be directed against both sexes, and whereas it has been directed against the poor only, we insist, and the working men insist, that it shall also apply to the rich profligate . . . It cannot be said there is no such thing as seduction of young girls by gentlemen of the upper classes. It cannot be said there is no such thing as profuse patronage of houses of ill fame by rich profligate men. . . . therefore we are profoundly convinced . . . that legislation, however pure its aim, which is directed against the weaker sex only, will fail to accomplish any reduction in the amount of misery and sin there is amongst us. That is the general outline of a series of measures, some of which it is intended to be proposed to the Legislature to adopt as legislative remedies. We have other remedies, especially with regard to increasing the number of industrial pursuits for women, which I should say is the most important, from the woman's side of the matter, but could hardly be touched, I suppose, by legislation.

The Times saw the failure of the Royal Commission as a vindication of its position. Its conclusion, set out in its leader of 20 July 1871, that the opponents of repeal had been vindicated was widely shared.

The Times, *20 July 1871*

A period of the Parliamentary Session has now been reached at which Ministers are advisedly lightening the ship by throwing overboard measures even of the most urgent practical importance. This, therefore, is not the time when the government can be expected to initiate legislation on a question so delicate and dubious as that involved in the Contagious Diseases Acts . . . We are well satisfied, therefore, with the reply given by the HOME SECRETARY to MR BAINES on Monday night, announcing the intention of the Government to postpone legislation for the present, and intimating that the substitution of a new Statute for those now in force is a matter requiring the 'deep and anxious consideration' of parliament. The Report of the Commission, which has just been published, appears to justify Mr Bruce's caution . . . Such consideration is most essential to any attempt at a settlement of this difficult subject. We cannot allow it to be disposed of on the mere Report of a Commission to which seven dissentients have been appended. The Report itself, although a useful document as a summary of the evidence, loses its weight when we learn that sixteen out of twenty-three Commissioners decline, in a greater or lesser degree, to assent to its practical recommendations. One thing, however, has been satisfactorily established by the inquiry. The illegitimate character of the agitation against the Acts, the groundless nature of the charges brought against their administration, and the mischievous tendency of the arguments popularly used by the advocates of their repeal, have been conclusively proved.

. . . It is very desirable that public men should make themselves acquainted with the evidence on which the Report is based before they determine how they will vote, should the question be raised next year. Seven members of the Commission sign a dissent, strongly urging the impolicy of the proposed repeal. Six members protest against the proposed revival of the Act of 1864. On such a divided judgement no action need be taken until those who are responsible for a change or an affirmation of a system which has achieved admirable sanitary results have arrived at an unbiased decision, after a full review of the evidence so laboriously gathered.

Gladstone's government did review the evidence carefully, and on 13 February 1872 Home Secretary Bruce introduced a Bill into the Commons which attempted to modify the law along the lines suggested by the Royal Commission. The measure predictably failed to satisfy either side. On 25 May 1872 *The Shield* expressed Repeal opinion at its most emotional, commenting 'It is scarcely possible any longer to doubt the treacherous policy of the Government . . . It is impossible to avoid the suspicion that they never meant to give repeal; and that they have hoped to kill the agitation against the Acts, by directing it to false issues.'

Meanwhile in May Bruce was confronted by nearly 150 MPs urging maintenance of the Acts in their existing form – 83 Tories and 63 Liberals. The Repealers could not muster anything like this cross-party strength. The weakness of the Repeal lobby in the Commons was shown on 9 July 1872 when Quaker Charles Gilpin brought in a Repeal Bill. The Bill was not even discussed, the House being counted out with only thirty-four MPs in the Chamber – six short of a quorum. *The Shield* responded with emotional intransigence.

The Shield, *20 July 1872*

Our readers are aware that when Mr Gilpin rose in the House of Commons . . . to move for leave to bring in a bill for the Repeal of the Contagious Diseases Acts, Mr Collins expressed his belief that there were not forty members present; the Speaker, after the usual interval, proceeded to count, and the result showed that there were only thirty-four representatives of the people ready, to allow this question to receive the light of discussion. . . .

We have never placed any faith in the actual House of Commons on this subject . . . We are aware that our strength is in the people, not in them. But it is important that the people should know – and by this test motion we have shown them – precisely of what stuff their so-called representatives are made. Henceforth the duty of our friends all over the country is clear. We can accept no compromise. We can support no half measures. The Government is directly hostile to us . . . From such a House of Commons there is nothing to hope, and we appeal from them to the constituencies. To those we would recall the old cry of the reformers of '32, 'New measures, new men' . . .

. . . Our strength is in the people; our appeal must be made to the people, and we believe the next general election will show that the people have learned the lesson so gallantly taught them by Mr Charles Gilpin.

Bruce concluded that the issue was a lost cause, and withdrew his Bill without debate on 15 July. Gladstone's Liberal Government thereafter took no interest in the Contagious Diseases Acts.

The intransigence of the extra-parliamentary wing of the Repeal Movement continued at the Pontefract by-election in August 1872. The Repealers challenged the popular Liberal candidate, H.C.E. Childers, financed by the Sheffield Liberal manufacturer, H.J. Wilson. There were scenes of violence similar to Colchester – at one point Josephine Butler and Mrs Wilson were trapped in a hayloft by roughs who tried to smoke them out – but the result was different. Childers had learnt from the defeat of Storks. He asserted in a letter to *The Times* that he had supported Bruce's bill as a half-way measure, apologised for the excesses of his supporters, and offered to prosecute any who could be identified. As a result his majority was reduced by the Repeal campaign – from 233 to 80 – but he held the seat.

The events at Colchester and Pontefract led the Repealers to overestimate their strength. What these by-elections showed was a significant but limited degree of support among Liberal voters for the Repeal Campaign. This was sufficient to reduce the Liberal vote, a strategy which could only help the Conservatives. As there was no significant support for Repeal among the Conservatives, the Repealers were thus achieving pyrrhic victories. This elementary political lesson was wholly missed in the declining years of Gladstone's first ministry. The effect of the Repeal strategy on the General Election of January–February 1874, if it had any effect at all, was to intensify the swing to the Conservatives and assist in defeating the Liberals. The Reformers found this lesson hard to grasp. *The Shield* was triumphalist:

The Shield, *28 February 1874*

The success which has attended our agitation during the General Election, ought to encourage the various Repeal Societies to equally vigorous action in those constituencies where new elections are about to take place. We have made our power felt during the recent contests to a degree and to an extent which has probably astonished our opponents more than ourselves . . . We have no trustworthy data upon which to calculate our chances of success at the hands of Mr Gladstone or Mr Disraeli; but we know that every member who can be brought to pledge himself for Repeal is an addition to the artillery with which we are laying siege to this immoral and unconstitutional legislation . . .

It is with especial earnestness that we call the attention of our friends to the contest now going forward in Oxford City. Mr Lewis, rejected by Devonport, on this question, is now offering himself to Oxford as Mr Cardwell's successor . . . He is a more dangerous foe to us than any dozen of his friends. Sensible of the importance of showing the country's feeling about the Acts, our Devonport supporters did not hesitate to bid him depart from their borough. His defeat has been felt in many quarters, and should he be rejected a second time by the determination of the electors of Oxford, our cause will gain an impetus which cannot be too highly estimated . . .

Lewis was indeed rejected by Oxford in favour of the Conservative, a result hailed by the Repealers as being due in part to their campaign. The more intelligent of Repealers then began to grasp the long-term consequences of such pyrrhic victories. The Repealers came to realise that they had lost large numbers of MPs who supported their cause. Fowler himself lost his seat, and rounded on the militants. At the Annual General Meeting of the Midland Counties Electoral Union – the Repeal Group for the Midlands – in December 1874, he condemned the policy of 'endeavouring to split up parties into small sections by undue pressure on candidates'. The anger of the MPs sank in and Josephine Butler suffered a nervous breakdown.

Campaigners struggled to find a successor to Fowler. Eventually in July 1874 the pro-reform MPs selected a new leadership, Sir Harcourt Johnstone and James Stansfeld, formerly president of the Local Government Board. Stansfeld, vice-chair of the National Association, was a figure of substance who directed strategy with an iron hand. He insisted that the extra-parliamentary wing be subordinated to the parliamentarians, and that parliamentary policy be directed to putting pressure on Disraeli's hostile ministry by procedural motions challenging the annual army estimates.

This was a limited strategy which bored MPs while neutralising the movement outside parliament. Conservative MP Henry Lucy defined an empty house as one in which 'Stansfeld was on his legs delivering his annual speech on the rights of his fellow women'. But however boring, after five weary years it bore fruit. On

17 March 1879, when C.H. Hopwood rose to move the annual ritual, Colonel Stanley for the Government forestalled him by announcing that the ministry would set up yet another select committee into the workings of the Acts (Hansard, 17 March 1879, col. 1039). Stansfeld and the MPs supporting him accepted with alacrity the chance to mobilise evidence against the Act.

The select committee was, however, no panacea. The repealers could only number five of the fifteen-member committee, while the cross-party lobby in favour of the Acts was powerful. Both Lord Cavendish Bentinck, judge advocate general in Disraeli's Conservative government, and his Liberal successor, George Osborne Morgan, supported the Acts. The Repealers calculated they had 179 supporters in the new parliament elected in 1880, with 232 MPs favouring regulation, and 241 MPs of unknown opinion. Stansfeld calculated that parliamentarians had to be carefully wooed and militancy outside parliament restrained.

The test of the strategy came in the summer of 1882. Three years of argument in committee had failed to produce a consensus, and the Committee produced a minority and majority report. Having marshalled their evidence, Repeal MPs prepared the ground for an attack on the Acts. Stansfeld won a ballot for a private member's bill in the Commons in the spring of 1883, and chose to move a motion not for repeal, but against the illiberality of state examination of women. His motion read 'That this House disapproves of the compulsory examination of women under the Contagious Diseases Acts'. He saw that this was the issue which most worried neutrals and which supporters of regulation found most difficult to justify.

Repealers focused intense pressure on Gladstone's cabinet. Under sustained attack from the non-conformist wing of the Liberal Party, the cabinet cracked, and made Stansfeld's resolution an open question. With the whips off, Stansfeld had a fighting chance. The debate, on 20 April 1883 was a long and exhaustive examination of both sides of the CD issue (Hansard, 20 April 1883, cols 749–857). At the end Stansfeld carried the day by 182 votes to 110. The Repealers were exultant. Yet the battle was far from over. The system had been wrecked, but the CD Acts remained on the statute book and supporters of regulation threatened to reinstate compulsory inspection if a change of government took place. *The Shield* commented:

The Shield, *5 May 1883*

The Government has taken Mr Stansfeld's resolution *au pied de la lettre*, has resolved on the withdrawal of the Acts police and the compulsory examination of women captured by them; but has drawn the line at this impossible point. If the proposals of the Government be carried out in future, 'Any woman voluntarily presenting herself at a certified hospital may, at her own request, be examined by a duly appointed surgeon; and if found diseased, may, on the certificate to that effect of such surgeon, be admitted into such hospital, and detained there *in accordance with the provisions of the present Acts.*'

In other words, the prison hospitals are to continue to exist, to continue to exist for one sex only; and women are in the future, as in the past, to be incarcerated, and submitted to enforced medical or surgical treatment, in order that they may be made healthy instruments of military and naval debauchery. It is true the women are 'voluntarily' to present themselves; but who that knows anything of 'voluntary' submission has any confidence in this? And that is not all. The threat – for we can take it as naught else – of a resuscitation of Mr Bruce's bill of 1872, is nothing less than an intimation of the extension of this monstrous system to the whole population – or rather the whole *female* population – of these islands. Our friends must be up and doing, or our last state may be worse than our first.

The suspicious tone was partly justified. While they had won a significant victory over the CD Acts and what they regarded as the vice lobby, the moral purity position on the CD laws was far from triumphant. Moral purity campaigners were quite right in fearing a return of Acts which had only been suspended, not repealed. However, they could have no inkling of the curious twists of fate through which their hopes of complete repeal would come to fruition.

9. *White Slavery and the 1885 Criminal Law Amendment Act*

While Stansfeld and his supporters were combating the CD Acts, a parallel campaign was developing, one which was to have far wider ranging consequences than a campaign to repeal a relatively obscure set of laws. In the early 1880s the issue of white slavery became a major scandal. Puritan campaigners had discovered that British women were being kept against their will in Continental brothels. Their campaign against this odious situation generated a highly explosive political situation. The issue became politically controversial when the following memorial arrived on the desk of the Liberal Foreign Secretary Earl Granville in early August 1880.

Memorial to the Foreign Secretary

The following Memorial (with Declarations in corroboration) has been laid before Earl Granville by the London Committee, for whose names see the end of the Memorial.

To the Right Honourable the Earl Granville, KG, Her Majesty's Principal Secretary of State for Foreign Affairs.

The memorial of the undersigned members of a Committee, formed in London for the purpose of exposing and suppressing the existing traffic in English, Scotch, and Irish Girls, for the Purpose of Foreign Prostitution,

Respectfully sheweth:

That there exists a system of systematic abduction, to Brussels and elsewhere on the Continent, of girls who are British subjects, for purposes of prostitution, and that the girls so abducted, being sold to the keepers of licensed houses of infamy, are generally confined and detained against their will in such houses.

Many of the girls so abducted are induced by men of respectable exterior to go abroad under promise of marriage or of obtaining employment or situations; and, on arrival there are taken to the office of the *Police des Moeurs* [Vice Police] for registration as prostitutes.

In most cases, the girls know nothing of the language or customs of the country, and are entirely ignorant of the system of registration of prostitutes which exists on the Continent, and of what is being transacted at the office aforesaid; and, before being taken there, they are often made to believe that the place is the Custom House, and that they are going there to comply with formalities required from travellers who arrive there from another country, and they are generally registered for reasons that are hereinafter stated, in false names.

According to the letter of the Belgian law, a woman may not be registered as a prostitute under the age of twenty-one years, but this legal rule is easily and most frequently evaded, for the purpose of securing young victims, by the following means: Any certificate of birth can be obtained in England, by any person whomsoever, on payment of a few shillings. The abductor, therefore, produces a true certificate of the birth of some female who has attained twenty-one years, and presents such certificate to the *Police des Moeurs* as that of the girls who is under age, and whom he wishes to register . . .

After a girl has been registered (with or without her knowledge or consent), and immured in a licensed house of prostitution, it is, in most cases, impossible for her to regain her freedom . . . The houses are constructed so as to prevent egress without the concurrence of the keepers thereof. Terrorism is also exercised over these girls, if any wish or attempt to escape is manifest; they are subjected to violence, and are intimidated by threats of the imprisonment to which they have become liable through being registered in a false name. They are also invariably kept in debt to the keepers of the tolerated houses, and these persons frequently sell the miserable girls from one house to another, that traces of them may be lost or rendered difficult . . .

A female British subject, who has been entrapped into, and is kept against her will in a *maison tolerée* in Brussels, is seldom allowed to go out of the house – never unless accompanied by a person in charge; and it has been found almost impossible for friends desiring to assist her, to obtain any help, either from the Belgian Police or the English Diplomatic or Consular authorities. Her condition is that of a slave to the lust of all who will pay the brothel-keeper's charge for permission to violate and outrage her, until disease renders her unprofitable, or death shall afford release.

Your Memorialists have made themselves acquainted with the cases of English, Scotch and Irish girls who have been decoyed into or detained in this horrible slavery; and some of your Memorialists have personally visited Brussels for that purpose, and have failed in releasing others . . .

Your Memorialists submit to your Lordship that such changes ought to be made in the English and Belgian law as shall make it impossible for any woman, who is a subject of Her Majesty the Queen to be deprived of her liberty by fraud or force, and to be kept in that country, in bondage for the vilest of purposes . . .

And your Memorialists crave your Lordship's powerful influence in favour of such measures as shall provide effectual and prompt release of those of Her Majesty's female subjects who have been decoyed into a foul slavery abroad, and whose forlorn, helpless, and utterly woeful conditions (as shown forth in the statement before mentioned), your Memorialists hope will enlist your Lordship's sympathy in the cause they thus venture to submit to your Lordship's consideration. And your Memorialists will ever pray, &c.

BENJAMIN SCOTT, Guildhall, London, Chamberlain of London.

R. COPE MORGAN, Publisher, Paternoster Buildings.

GEORGE GILLETT, Banker, 72 Lombard St, E.C.

ALFRED S. DYER, Publisher, Amen Corner, Paternoster Row, London.

SEPTIMUS R. SCOTT, Old Broad Street, Chairman of Committee of Stock Exchange.

MARY STEWARD, Ongar, Essex.

MARY H.L. BUNTING, Endsleigh Gardens, Euston Square.

E. PHILIP BASTIN, West Drayton, Middlesex.

T.L. BOYD, Amhurst Lodge, Tunbridge Wells.

WM. PAYNE, Kennington Road, London.

London, August 5th 1880

This memorial arose out of a remarkable investigation by Alfred Dyer, a Quaker puritan activist, who had visited Brussels in 1879 and 1880 to investigate white slavery. The memorial given above was appended to Dyer's description of his discoveries, and published in the summer of 1880. Dyer had been conducting a press campaign on the subject since the start of the year. He encountered a wall of scepticism and indifference, but his efforts were to reap a whirlwind. His 1880 pamphlet, from which this extract is taken, was a ground-breaking text on white slavery in Europe, entitled *The European Slave Trade in English Girls*, published by the Dyer Brothers of Amen Corner, Paternoster Row, London, in 1880.

The European Slave Trade, *pp. 3–34*

In order properly to understand the subject of the foreign slave traffic in English girls, it is necessary to know something of the system of slavery, which this traffic exists to supply with victims.

In nearly every country on the Continent of Europe, prostitution is licensed by the public authorities . . . houses devoted to prostitution are licensed . . . and their inmates are forbidden to appear alone on the streets . . . The female inmates of houses of prostitution are in a state of virtual slavery . . . From the day they enter these houses they are not allowed to wear their own clothing, but are forced to accept garments of a disgusting nature, for the hire of which, and also for everything they require, they are charged exorbitant prices. They are thus kept deeply in debt . . . They are frequently brutally treated and beaten if they show any signs of insubordination . . . Moreover, as the letter of the law forbids the reception of girls who are minors, such girls are registered by their buyers or betrayers under false names with false certificates of birth, with or without the connivance of the officials, for which registration the girls are liable to imprisonment for forgery – a penalty which the keepers of the houses hold over them as a means of maintaining them in subjection . . .

The beginning of my personal knowledge of the condition . . . I have described was towards the close of last year [1879]. On leaving the Friends Meeting House, Clerkenwell, London, one Sabbath evening, one of my friends told me he had heard that a young English girl was confined in a licensed house of prostitution in Brussels, and was contemplating suicide as the only means of escape from her awful condition. I found on enquiry that his informant, a man of some position in London, had actually visited the house a few weeks previously, and although this girl implored him with tears to aid her to escape, he left her to her fate, probably fearing that any attempt at her escape would end in publicity, and thus compromise his reputation . . .

On receiving this information, friends in Brussels were at once communicated with, and with some difficulty the girl was found in hospital . . . Through the persevering agency of Pastor Leonard Anet, of Brussels, she was eventually returned to London, where I met her and received a corroboration of the foregoing story from her own lips . . . On the second day of the new year (1880) . . . I published the facts of her case in a letter to several London daily newspapers, together with the statement of another case that I had recently received from Brussels. This latter was as follows . . .

'On Thursday 16th October, Mr —, a lieutenant of Artillery, . . . was walking along the Rue — . . . He saw a gathering of people . . . In the midst of them was a young girl weeping bitterly and declaring aloud that she had that moment made her escape from the house of prostitution, No 28, Rue —, into which she had been decoyed against her will. The girl, who did not speak a word of French, affirmed that she was deceived in London by a Belgian agent who engaged to bring her to Holland, where he had found a place for her, he said, as

A French child prostitute. (Felicien Rops. Mary Evans Picture Library)

governess in a good family . . . Instead of keeping his promise, this agent had brought her straight to that house, where she had been forcibly detained until that hour. Mr —, and some other gentlemen . . . moved by pity, subscribed on the spot a little sum of money to place her in a safe shelter, because the keeper of the house was already loudly claiming her back. To this end they took her to a neighbouring hotel of good character . . . Shortly afterwards an individual appeared, openly declaring himself to have been sent there by the *police judiciare*, and politely invited the young girl to accompany him to the police office to give her evidence on the sad affair. This individual proved to be another of the gentlemanly agents of the houses of prostitution, and took the girl straight off and securely lodged her in another house of infamy, where she now is.'

In pursuance of my determination to further investigate the subject of the European slave trade in English girls, and at the request of a Committee which has now been formed in London to deal with the matter, I started for Brussels at the close of the second month of the present year. A week later, after acquiring considerable information about the system of regulated debauchery . . . I entered a house in that street, and saw a young Englishwoman of whom I had previously heard that she was anxious to escape. I entered into conversation with her in a room devoted to drinking. To avoid the object of my visit being suspected, I ordered some wine, which being a total abstainer I did not drink . . .

On my saying that I would aid her to escape, she appeared overcome with joy, which, however, was in a few minutes dispelled by an apparent sense of agonised bewilderment as she began to realise her true position. She pointed out to me that she could not leave in the clothing she had on; that though she had a box of good clothes of her own upstairs, she could not get at them then; and that moreover, if I were to endeavour to aid her to leave, such violence would be used as would probably frustrate her escape, and I should be half-killed in the attempt. Eventually, she begged me to come on the following morning, when she would have her own clothes ready, and make the endeavour to get away . . .

[The following morning] . . . Accompanied by Dr Alexis Splingard as a witness, and by my London friend, I proceeded to the house . . . The mistress was standing with another woman in the hall, her face white with rage. We asked to be allowed to see the young Englishwoman . . . The mistress replied, in tones clearly intimating a menace, 'You shall not see her; and for your advice, let me tell you not to come here again, for you will not be well received.' . . . Being refused an interview we left the house, but had scarcely walked thirty yards, when a great brutal looking fellow ran and overtook us, and shaking his fist . . . exclaimed that if we three came to that house again he would break the heads of all three of us . . .

Feeling now that the very life of this woman was perhaps insecure, I went to the residence of the British Minister to claim the protection of British authority for a woman who, notwithstanding her imprisonment in a licensed house of ill fame, was a British subject . . . He said that the matter was more in the department of Thos E. Jeffs, the Pro-Consul . . . I drove to the residence of the Pro-Consul, who said he would communicate with the proper authorities. Subsequently, he stated that he would see the girl himself. I appealed to him also to have her removed at once from the house in which she then was, to some place of safety, and I said that no investigation into her statement could be satisfactory while she remained in that house. He answered that he had no power to have her removed . . .

The result was as I feared . . . Three Belgian functionaries, including their own interpreter, and wholly unaccompanied by any representative of the British Embassy, went to the house where the young woman was detained, and conducted what I cannot but term a sham investigation . . . She was brought into their presence by the brothel keeper, and these men, strangers to her . . . commenced to put a series of cold official questions . . . It is not surprising that she replied to these foreign functionaries in a way that seemed likely to preserve her from the unknown horrors of another fate. This one-sided investigation; this examination of a cowed and terrified girl in the house from which she wished but feared to escape; this enquiry without the presence of one impartial witness; this judicial farce was afterwards quoted by the Procureur du Roi in the *Journal de Bruxelles*, as a conclusive refutation of my statement that the young woman was detained in a life of infamy against her will . . .

The same day I entered several other licensed houses of prostitution, and saw other English girls who were either anxious or willing to escape, but who were intimidated from doing so . . .

This is the sort of thing which has been going on un-revealed, under cover of the system of regulated debauchery . . . It is impossible for it to be administered without corrupting the officials engaged in its execution . . . and thus atrocities become possible such as ordinary English men and women would never dream of.

Unhappily, however, the British public are easily misled by official assurances. When I first revealed in the London daily newspapers, the existence of the infamous traffic in our own flesh and blood, which has called forth this pamphlet . . . a letter appeared in the London daily newspapers from the British Pro-Consul at Brussel, the closing words of which were – 'From the experience I have gained in thoroughly investigating these and other similar cases, I can confidently assure the parents of all really "virtuous girls" that there is no fear whatever of finding their children in the same position as the girls referred to in Mr Dyer's letter.'

I am sorry for the sake of the Pro-Consul . . . for of all the officials on whom I called in Brussels, he was the one who bore the most respectable reputation. By this time he has probably learnt how grossly he was deceived . . .

. . . there is no measure that the human mind can conceive, that can provide against the corruption that is the inevitable concomitant of the system of legalised debauchery . . . The British public will probably hear a great deal from Brussels, not only of precautions to prevent girls entering houses of prostitution against their will, but also of the facilities (!) which the authorities there afford to girls to leave such houses. We have seen how those facilities work . . .

These slave traders in British girls have been for years carrying on their business under the eyes and with the knowledge of the Metropolitan detective police . . . Why then has the matter not been pressed on the attention of the Government before? It may be true that the head of the Metropolitan detective force and other high officials wish the Continental system of regulated debauchery to be introduced into Great Britain . . . but is it possible that the people of this kingdom will allow the private wishes of police and other functionaries . . . to override the interests of justice, mercy and liberty? . . . Let the old anti-slavery spirit speak out.

Dyer's pamphlet was suffused with suppressed passion, but his narrative was accurate and proved an effective account of a real scandal later corroborated by independent investigation. Moral purity campaigners rapidly backed him. Josephine Butler, in *The Shield* of 1 May 1880, alleged that 'In certain of the infamous houses in Brussels there are immured little children, English girls of from ten to fourteen years of age, who have been stolen, kidnapped, betrayed, carried off from English country villages by every artifice, and sold to these human shambles. The presence of these children is unknown to the ordinary visitors; it is secretly known only to the wealthy men who are able to pay large sums of money for the sacrifice of these innocents.' The allegation of child prostitution was to become an article of faith among the moral purity lobby, and to emerge with explosive force in the 'Maiden Tribute' campaign of 1885.

Yet it was never easy for the moral purity campaign to establish the truth of the allegation. Josephine Butler's allegations of child prostitution were temporarily forgotten as she became embroiled in a dispute over police corruption. Puritan allegations of corruption of the Belgian vice police by brothel owners were sensationally vindicated by a successful court case in Brussels in December. The chief and second in command of the Brussels morals police, Lenaers and Scroeder, were dismissed.

The moral puritans were convinced that they faced a vice conspiracy on both sides of the Channel. The Granville Memorial received only a cold formal acknowledgement, and the puritans concluded it had been ignored. During the winter of 1880/1, it appeared to the reform lobby that Whitehall was indifferent to their concerns. This was not so. Granville had decided that a proper investigation was needed, conducted by an official separate from the police establishment. In December 1880 a conscientous barrister from the Middle Temple, Thomas Snagge, was quietly despatched to Belgium. Snagge's report in the spring of 1881 demonstrated conclusively that the abuses detailed by Dyer were no figment of a fevered imagination. But his report was secret, and puritan letters received no more than a formal reply. Furious, Josephine Butler raised a petition calling for 'Such changes . . . in the English laws as should make it impossible for any young girl or child in our country to be deprived of her liberty by fraud or violence, and to be kept in a foreign city in bondage . . .' . She presented it to Granville in person, and was pleasantly surprised to find that the government was preparing to move for a select committee of the House of Lords to investigate white slavery.

The Earl of Dalhousie moved the motion for a select committee on 30 May 1881 (Hansard, cols 1603–1609). He presented an overwhelming case for the appointment of the investigative committee. His speech, from which extracts are given below, was, however, cleverly crafted to give the impression that the whole issue had arisen through long-standing government concerns. The purity lobby found themselves excluded from the official record. Nevertheless, there is no doubt that it was their efforts which had securing the select committee.

The law relating to the protection of young girls

Motion for a Select Committee
The Earl of Dalhousie, in rising to move 'That a Select Committee be appointed to inquire into the state of the law relative to the protection of young girls from artifices to induce them to lead a corrupt life, and into the means of amending the same', said the subject had from time to time occupied the attention of the Government for a number of years past. Several series of correspondence had taken place between the Foreign Office and our

Diplomatic and Consular Agents in Belgium and Antwerp. The first occurred in 1874, and related to certain English girls who had been decoyed to Antwerp under false pretences . . . one of them, who was kept there against her will, wrote a very touching and pathetic letter to the English Consul asking him to come and see her, in order that she might tell him her story . . . It was then forwarded through the Home Office to the Secretary of State for Foreign Affairs . . . After investigation, one of the girls was found in hospital. The second, the Consul reported, declined to be sent home, and the third, who had written the letter, had left clandestinely, and it was not known where she had gone. In fact, nothing more was ever heard of her again . . .

Another correspondence took place in 1876 with respect to certain English girls who had been decoyed over to Antwerp; but in that case the English chaplain stepped in and frustrated the abominable purpose for which they had been brought over. Nothing more occurred until May 1879, when the Consul at Antwerp reported to the Foreign Office in London that a well known procurer named Klyber had been convicted in Belgium of decoying English girls under age and sentenced to imprisonment for having infringed the law; but the man stated at the trial, what was the fact, that his doings were perfectly legal in England. There was no further correspondence util the year 1880.

On the 3rd June the Secretary of State for Foreign Affairs communicated with the Home Office, and suggested that a police agent should be sent to Brussels to make inquiries. This was accordingly done, but with very little result; for after making inquiries at Rotterdam, Antwerp, Calais, and Boulogne, the police agent reported that he had only found two English girls who had been decoyed away by false pretences . . .

In September the noble Earl the Secretary of State for Foreign Affairs suggested to the Home Office that an inquiry should be made by some person unconnected either with the police or with any government office. The gentlemen selected for this duty was a very well known and very able member of the English bar, Mr Snagge. Mr Snagge . . . had the advantage of speaking French perfectly, made a full and exhaustive inquiry, both at Antwerp and Brussels . . . Mr Snagge was . . . able to establish the fact that there were upwards of 20 procurers who had been at work to the knowledge of the police ever since 1865. The number of English girls decoyed to the Continent by these wretches they should never know . . . There was no doubt whatever that the business was a very large one, and that many respectable girls were thus ruined . . .

Among the cases mentioned by Mr Snagge, one young woman was engaged to enter a hotel, another was engaged as an actress, and a third, perfectly innocent, was sent from Brussels to Antwerp, there violated, then returned to

Brussels and entered on the public register. A fourth died at home in England from the treatment she had received. A fifth was deliberately seduced in England for the purpose of placing her in a registered house abroad. In these houses the women were treated as valuable cattle; they had plenty to eat and drink, and dissipation of all kinds was resorted to with the object of reconciling them to their mode of life. In theory the women were free . . . but practically they were captives, ignorant of the language of the people they were among. The head of the establishment kept the key to the front door; and the inmates were shown to be heavily in debt to the keeper, by a ledger account over which they had no control, beginning actually with the levy to the procurer for decoying them away. It was captivity of the most abominable kind. With regard to the English law on the subject, there was no doubt, as it stood at the present, that these procurers could ply their trade in the streets of London and elsewhere with perfect security . . .

Mr Snagge had taken some pains to devise a remedy, and his suggestion was that there should be a short enactment passed making it a criminal offence to entice anyone to become a common prostitute, whether within the Queen's Dominions or not. That, however, would be a matter for the Select Committee to determine . . .

It was no longer a matter of doubt that for some years past a large number of English girls, some of whom were perfectly innocent, had been annually exported to supply the demand of foreign brothels. . . . there could be no doubt that, during the last 15 years, many Englishwomen had, against their will, endured a life of worse than living death, from which there was no escape, within the walls of a foreign brothel . . . He had said enough, and he felt sure that their Lordships would be of opinion that no time should be lost in putting an end to a practice which, in arrant villany and rascality, surpassed all that they knew of any other trade in human beings, and in any other part of the world, either in ancient or modern times. He begged to make the motion which stood in his name.

The select committee was duly approved, and took evidence in the summer of 1881, continuing to the summer of 1882, and making an exhaustive interrogation of witnesses. The inquiry did not confine itself to the Continent, but examined the British end of the trade. In this context the evidence given by Howard Vincent, director of the Criminal Investigation Department of the Metropolitan Police, was of the greatest importance to moral reformers in Britain. The evidence relating to child prostitution in London is presented below. Vincent was interviewed on 19 July 1881.

Howard Vincent's evidence to the Select Committee

557. (Chairman) You are Director of Criminal Investigations are you not?

I am.

558. Has it happened that your attention has been called to one of the subjects which this committee is inquiring into, namely, the taking of young girls from England to foreign countries for the purposes of prostitution?

It has.

559. Have you known of many such cases?

I have known of several such cases.

560. Were the cases which you knew of: were they brought before you for the purpose of obtaining redress?

They were not brought before me by the individuals themselves; my attention was directed to them, partly by instructions from the Secretary of State, partly by foreign police authorities, partly by letters from Mrs Butler, Mr Dyer and other persons interested in the subject. Communication was entered into with the police of the countries concerned, and the steps were taken, as your Lordships are aware, with the approval of the Secretary of State.

561. Did this happen during the last few years?

This is within the last two years . . .

567. Has your attention been called to the subject generally of juvenile prostitution in London?

Very much so indeed.

568. Using the term 'juvenile' to apply to the prostitution of girls under 21, does it prevail largely in London?

In no city in Europe to so large an extent, in my opinion.

569. Down to what age?

Down to the statutory limit of 13; there is no protection in the present state of the law for girls over 13 years of age . . .

579. To return to the subject of juvenile prostitution, where are these children of 13 years and upwards to be found?

There are houses in London, in many parts of London, where there are people who will procure children for the purposes of immorality and prostitution, without any difficulty whatsoever above the age of 13, children without number at 14, 15 and 16 years of age. Superintendent Dunlap will tell you that juvenile prostitution is rampant at this moment, and that in the streets about the Haymarket, Waterloo Place, and Piccadilly, from nightfall there are children of 14, 15 and 16 years of age, going about openly soliciting prostitution . . . this prostitution actually takes place with the knowledge and connivance of the mother and to the profit of the household. I am speaking of some facts within my own knowledge, from hearsay, of course, but I have no reason whatever to doubt them. These procuresses . . . have an understanding with the mother of the girl that she shall come to that house at a certain hour, and the mother perfectly well knows for what purpose she goes there, and it is with her knowledge and connivance, and with her consent that the girl goes . . .

591. (Chairman) Do you know whether the police are able to trace these children as they get older, and to know what becomes of them?

I am afraid not. The police are absolutely powerless as regards prostitution in London.

592. With regard to children of this age, or any age, who are soliciting prostitution in the streets, have the police no power at all?

No power whatever.

593. (Lord Aberdare.) Only to keep order?

Only to keep order; and the consequence is that the state of affairs which exists in this capital is such that from four o'clock, or one may say from three o'clock in the afternoon, it is impossible for any respectable woman to walk from the top of the Haymarket to Wellington Street, Strand. From three or four o'clock in the afternoon, Villiers Street and Charing Cross Station, and the Strand, are crowded with prostitutes, who are there openly soliciting prostitution in broad daylight. At half past twelve at night, a calculation was made a short time ago that there was 500 prostitutes between Piccadilly Circus and the bottom of Waterloo-place.

594. Open solicitation in the streets is an offence against the law is it not?

Yes, it is an offence, but the police are powerless to do anything, because it must be to the annoyance and obstruction of passengers, and no respectable person is willing to go into a police court and say they were solicited by prostitutes . . .

616. (Chairman.) What is the technical definition of prosecution of a brothel; is it a place frequented by prostitutes?

That is the definition of a brothel or bawdy house . . . To keep such to the annoyance of any two inhabitants who will prosecute as a common nuisance, is a misdemeanour punishable by fine and imprisonment; that is under the common law.

617. (Lord Norton.) What can the vestry do?

Complaint can be preferred against any disorderly house by any two inhabitants who make the information upon oath, and enter into their recognizances to prosecute.

618. (Lord Aberdare.) I think the local authorities have power to prosecute at the public expense?

That is the case; but your Lordship will see that it is absolutely necessary to have two inhabitants; it is exceedingly difficult to find two inhabitants to come forward to prosecute a brothel.

619. It is generally done with a view of clearing the immediate neighbourhood of houses either offensive to themselves, or detracting from the value of their property?

That is, no doubt, the case. I mention this more particularly as to the police knowledge of these matters; the police have so little power of dealing with prostitutes or brothels, that they know very little about them . . .

640. (Chairman.) What is the power of the police with regard to the solicitation to prostitution in the streets; supposing they see some of these children, or young girls, soliciting men in the streets, what can they do?

Absolutely nil.

641. (Lord Aberdare.) I suppose they could go to the man solicited, and ask him if he would assist in preventing the nuisance, by giving evidence that these girls had annoyed him?

Yes, but I am afraid that people would not do it, or favourably regard the preferment of the request.

642. (Chairman.) Is it defined to be an offence by law, to solicit men in the streets?

Here is the section of the Police Act, the 2nd and 3rd Victoria, chapter 47; it is the 11th subsection of Section 54; 'Every common prostitute or night walker loitering or being in any thoroughfare or public place for the purpose of prostitution or solicitation to the annoyance of the inhabitants or passengers.'

643. (Lord Aberdare.) It can hardly be said then if they sought it that it was 'done to their annoyance'?
    That is so.

644. The words relate not only to the persons solicited, but to the annoyance of the inhabitants?
    Yes . . .

646. (Chairman.) Passing from the present state of the law, which you say is very imperfect and insufficient, has it occurred to you in what way the law could be strengthened to cope with this great evil that you speak of, especially juvenile prostitution?
    I anticipated your Lordship's question, and I have drawn a draft bill, which is very crude, but I have drawn it up to put forward my views in succinct form. I will read it, but I should like to make one observation first of all, and that is, that I do not think the evil of juvenile prostitution is entirely confined to females. I think it is applicable to a very large extent indeed to males. I mean that everything centering in London, as it does in this country . . . everybody sends their sons up to London necessarily for examination; and a boy must be a paragon of virtue, who, at 16 or 17, can walk . . . from the top of the Haymarket to the top of Grosvenor Place, without being solicited to such an enormous extent that he is almost certain to fall . . . If your Lordship will allow me I will read the bill. . . .

The evidence of Vincent and those who felt like him, and the impartial evidence provided by Thomas Snagge, convinced their Lordships that a serious situation existed, and that the law was inadequate to deal with the problems revealed by their enquiry. They therefore recommended that the law be tightened. The key points were as follows.

Report of the Select Committee of the House of Lords on the law relating to the protection of young girls, 10 July 1882

1. That it be made a serious misdemeanour for any person to solicit or endeavour to procure any woman to leave the United Kingdom, or to leave her usual place of abode in the United Kingdom, for the purpose of entering a

brothel, or prostituting herself, in parts beyond the seas, whether he shall or shall not inform the woman of such purpose.

3. That the age up to which it shall be an offence to have, or attempt to have carnal knowledge of, or to indecently assault a girl, be raised from 13 to 16.

4. That the age of unlawful abduction (24 & 25 Vic. c. 100, s. 55), with intent to have carnal knowledge unlawfully, be raised from 16 to 21.

5. That it shall be a misdemeanour for any person to receive into any house or into or on to any premises occupied or possessed by him, or of which he has the management or control, any girl under the age of 16 years for the purpose of her having unlawful sexual intercourse with any person, whether such intercourse is intended with any particular man or generally.

7. That the soliciting of prostitution in the public streets be made an offence and the police authorised to act accordingly, without proof that it is done 'to the annoyance of inhabitants or passengers'.

8. That the police be authorised to make applications, under the Industrial Schools Amendment Act, 1880, as to the children therein mentioned, and that any magistrate before whom a girl under the age of 16 is convicted of soliciting prostitution, may, if it shall appear that she has no friends able to provide a suitable home for her, remit her to a refuge or industrial home until she attains the age of 16.

Their Lordships had left Gladstone's government with no alternative but to legislate on an indefensible state of affairs. Accordingly, a bill was drafted and introduced into the Lords by Lord Rosebery on 31 May 1883. Rosebery was important, and his moving of the first reading of the Criminal Law Amendment Bill was a sign that it had cabinet support. But it was hardly overwhelming cabinet support. The actual steering of the Bill was left to the more junior Earl of Dalhousie, whose labours were to be exceedingly trying.

The Criminal Law Amendment Bill was a sickly infant. The original Bill suffered serious criticism on the second reading, experienced a serious mauling in committee on 29 June, and despite passing the third reading on 5 July was promptly withdrawn. Gladstone's ministers seem to have reasoned that if the Bill had struggled in the Lords, which had its own select committee report to back the Bill, then it had little chance of passing the Commons.

Dalhousie returned in the spring of 1884 with a much weaker Bill. Dalhousie referred explicitly to the need to propitiate public opinion, which many of their Lordships had argued would not support too puritan a measure. The weaker Bill duly passed the Lords, but not before the obscure Lord Oranmore and Brown sounded an ominous note. He commented that 'he believed that there were very few of their Lordships who had not, when young men, been guilty of immorality. He hoped that they would pause before passing a clause within the range of which their sons might come . . .' He was expressing with unusual candour precisely the hypocritical double standard which most infuriated puritans.

The second Bill was moved in the Commons by the Home Secretary, Sir William Harcourt, on 3 July 1884. But the Liberals had higher priorities, and it was dropped on 10 July. Dalhousie was forced to come back to the Lords with a third, and even weaker measure, in the spring of 1885. It passed through its readings in the House of Lords, but critics argued that with Gladstone's government in serious trouble, the chances of a controversial law passing the Commons were minimal. Their views were justified. When Harcourt moved the second reading of the third Bill on 22 May 1885, the day before the Whitsun adjournment, he spoke to an almost empty house. Cavendish-Bentinck, the notorious Tory reactionary, demanded that the house be counted. A bare quorum – forty members – were shown to be in the chamber. The speaker promptly adjourned the debate amid much bad tempered, end of term bickering. With most MPs expecting Gladstone to resign and call a General Election, observers expected the Bill to fall with the Government.

This prospect profoundly depressed one puritan observer of the debate, Benjamin Scott. Scott was Chair of the London Committee for the Exposure and Suppression of the Traffic in English Girls and had signed the memorial to Granville in 1880. Realising that five years' work was in danger of falling with Gladstone, Scott immediately turned to the Bill's one firm press supporter, the *Pall Mall Gazette*. Scott visited its campaigning puritan editor, W.T. Stead, and convinced him that he must take up the cause. Stead was initially sceptical of success in securing the passage of the Criminal Law Amendment Bill before a General Election could be called, but saw a small window of opportunity if the election were delayed.

The events which followed were thus only possible because of a parliamentary hiatus. Gladstone's failing government staggered on till 8 June, when an amendment to the budget was carried and Gladstone resigned. No General Election followed, however, as the new electoral registers were not ready. Lord Salisbury formed a minority Conservative administration on 24 June. Stead and Scott knew that while the interregnum lasted, the Criminal Law Amendment Bill was politically alive. Yet debate on the Bill stood adjourned, with the Tories having no interest in reopening it. Stead concluded that to force its passage would require a sensation so strong that the most indifferent ministry would have no choice but to pass the Bill. He set out to produce such a sensation. He set up a 'Secret Commission', including Josephine Butler and the leaders of the Salvation Army, which was well known for its work among prostitutes. The task of the 'Secret Commission' was quietly to gather evidence on child prostitution and related scandals, which Stead could use as ammunition. By early July, Stead was ready to publish. On Saturday 4 July the following appeared on the front page of the *Pall Mall Gazette* [eio].

Notice to our Readers

A Frank Warning

The Criminal Law Amendment Bill, it is said, will be abandoned, owing to the late period of the session and the difficulty of finding time to carry it through the Commons. That measure deals with a subject the importance of which has been admitted by both parties, and is based upon the urgent recommendations of a House of Lords Committee of which Lord Salisbury was a member. It has thrice been passed through the House of Lords, and now for the third time it is threatened with extinction in the House of Commons. . . . But if Ministers think of allowing the Bill to drop because the public is not keenly alive to its importance, it is necessary to open the eyes of the public, in order that a measure the urgency of which has been repeatedly admitted may pass into law this session. *We have, therefore, determined, with a full sense of the responsibility attaching to such a decision, to publish the report of a Special and Secret Commission of Inquiry which we appointed to examine into the whole subject.* It is a long, detailed report, dealing with those phases of sexual criminality which the Criminal Law Amendment Bill was framed to repress. Nothing but the most imperious sense of public duty would justify its publication. But as we are assured on every hand, on the best authority, that without its publication the Bill will be abandoned for the third time, we dare not face the responsibility of its suppression. We shall, therefore, begin its publication on Monday. . . . We have no desire to inflict upon unwilling eyes the ghastly story of the criminal developments of modern vice. Therefore we say quite frankly today that all those who are squeamish, and all those who are prudish, and all those who prefer to live in a fool's paradise of imaginary innocence and purity . . . will do well not to read the *Pall Mall Gazette* of Monday and the three following days. The story of an actual pilgrimage into a real hell is not pleasant reading, and it is not meant to be. It is, however, an authentic record of unimpeachable facts, 'abominable, unutterable, and worse than fables yet have feigned or fear conceived.' But it is true, and its publication is necessary.

With this melodramatic and distinctly salacious warning, Stead set out his stall. The title he chose for his articles – 'The Maiden Tribute of Modern Babylon' – was selected to remind the classically trained among his readers of the legend of the sacrifice of virgins to the Minotaur. Stead was comparing the ultra-respectability of straitlaced Victorian London to the corruption of ancient Babylon. On 6 July he launched a dramatic and self-congratulatory exposé of London vice on to the streets of London calculating, correctly, that he would produce a sensation no government could ignore.

The Maiden Tribute of Ancient Babylon

The Report of our Secret Commission, pp. 1–3

In ancient times, if we may believe the myths of Hellas, Athens . . . was compelled by her conqueror to send once every nine years a tribute to Crete of seven youths and seven maidens. The doomed fourteen, who were selected by lot amid the lamentations of the citizens, returned no more . . . This very night in London, and every night, year in and year out, not seven maidens only, but many times seven . . . Maidens they will be when this morning dawned, but tonight their ruin will be accomplished, and to-morrow they will find themselves within the portals of the maze of London brotheldom . . . Many, no doubt, who venture but a little way into the maze make their escape. But multitudes are swept irresistibly on and on to be destroyed in due season, to give place to others, who also will share their doom . . .

I am not without hope that there may be some check placed upon this vast tribute of maidens, unwitting and unwilling, which is nightly levied in London by the vices of the rich upon the necessities of the poor. London's lust annually uses up many thousands of women, who are literally killed and made away with – living sacrifices slain in the service of vice. That may be inevitable, and with that I have nothing to do. But I do ask that those doomed to the house of evil fame shall not be trapped into it unwillingly, and that none shall be beguiled into the chamber of death before they are of an age to read the inscription above the portal – 'abandon hope all ye who enter here' . . .

That crime of the most ruthless and abominable description is constantly and systematically practised in London without let or hindrance, I am in a position to prove from my personal experience. . . . These crimes may be roughly classified as follows:

I.   The sale and purchase and violation of children.

II.   The procuration of virgins.

III.   The entrapping and ruin of women.
IV.   The international slave trade in girls.
V.   Atrocities, brutalities, and unnatural crimes.

When the Criminal Law Amendment Bill was talked out just before the defeat of the Ministry . . . I undertook an investigation into the facts . . . For four weeks, aided by two or three coadjutors of whose devotion and self sacrifice . . . I cannot speak too highly, I have been exploring the London Inferno . . . The facts which I and my coadjutors have verified I now place on record at once as a revelation and a warning – a revelation of the system, and a warning to those who may be its victims. . . .

Stead then went into a detailed study of the five classes of sexual 'crime' which he had detailed in his introduction. There were many sensations, but the one which stood out was the apparent confirmation of the worst abuse alleged by the moral purity lobby, the rape of young girls. This was the story of 'Lily', which Stead used to climax his first article.

A Child of Thirteen bought for £5
At the beginning of Derby week, a woman . . . entered a brothel in — St. M—, kept by an old acquaintance, and opened negotiations for the purchase of a maid . . . While the negotiations were going on, a drunken neighbour came into the house . . . So far from being horrified at the proposed sale of the girl, she whispered eagerly to the seller, 'Don't you think she would take our Lily? I think she would suit.' Lily was her own daughter, a bright, fresh-looking little girl, who was thirteen years old. The bargain, however, was made for the other child, and Lily's mother felt she had lost her market . . . Then came the chance of Lily's mother. The brothel-keeper sent for her, and offered her a sovereign for her daughter. The woman was poor, dissolute and indifferent to everything but drink. Her father, who was also a drunken man, was told his daughter was going to a situation . . . The brothel keeper, having secured possession of the child, then sold her to the procuress . . . for £5 – £3 paid down, and the remaining £2 after her virginity had been professionally certified. The little girl . . . was told she must go with this strange woman to a situation . . .
    The first thing to be done after the child was fairly secured from home was to secure the certificate of virginity without which the rest of the purchase money would not be forthcoming. In order to avoid trouble she was taken in a cab to the house of a mid-wife . . . the examination was very brief, and completely satisfactory . . . From the midwife's the innocent girl was taken to a

house of ill fame . . . where, notwithstanding her extreme youth, she was admitted without question. She was taken upstairs, undressed, and put to bed, the woman who brought her putting her to sleep. She was rather restless, but under the influence of chloroform she soon went over. Then the woman withdrew. All was quiet and still. A few moments later the door opened and the purchaser entered the bedroom. He closed and locked the door. There was a brief silence. And then there rose a wild and piteous cry . . . and the child's voice was heard crying, in accents of terror, 'There's a man in the room! Take me home; Oh, take me home!' And then all once more was still.

This story was deeply questionable – Stead did not reveal that he was the purchaser, and that the implication of rape was unfounded, but the impact was immediate and unquestioned. By the afternoon of Tuesday 7 July, as the second article was going to press, demand for the *Pall Mall Gazette* was so great that a black market had developed. The *St James Gazette* led a chorus of respectable press disapproval attacking not the situation Stead had described, but Stead's temerity in revealing it. At question time in the Commons, Cavendish-Bentinck asked the Home Secretary, Richard Cross, whether the *Pall Mall Gazette* could be subjected to criminal prosecution. Cross replied non-committally that 'the publication can be dealt with by indictment in the usual way'. He was uncomfortably aware that a major scandal was developing.

By Wednesday crowds round Stead's offices in Northumberland street were so large and unruly that his staff barricaded themselves in. In that day's editorial, Stead raised the stakes by threatening to expose the patrons of high class London brothels – including royalty – from the witness box if he were prosecuted. It was a threat Salisbury's government took very seriously indeed. The ministry decided to run before a gathering storm. On Thursday 9 July the Home Secretary rose in the Commons to resume the second reading of the Criminal Law Amendment Bill adjourned at Whitsun. He naturally did not refer to the *Pall Mall Gazette*'s press campaign.

Over the next month, the government's law officers toiled over an increasingly complex piece of legislation while Stead and his allies kept up the pressure. Massive demonstrations of support were held in cities as far apart as Portsmouth, Manchester and Newcastle upon Tyne. On 30 July a petition organised by the Salvation Army and containing 393,000 signatures,was taken to parliament accompanied by hundreds of Salvation Army officers. The same day, Cross told MPs in Committee that 'We shall go on with the consideration of the measure from day to day until the Committee is closed. This is a question which has stirred England from one end to the other . . .' His assessment was correct. The Bill passed the Committee stage and the second and third readings in the Commons by

7 August, passed the Lords on the 10th, and received the Royal Assent on the 14th. For a Bill which had effectively been dead at Whitsun, this was a remarkable change of fortune.

As passed, the Criminal Law Amendment Act of 1885 embodied all the major recommendations of the Lords Select Committee of 1882, and satisfied all the major demands of the moral purity lobby. The main provisions are given below. Stead was a curiously flawed character, and his triumph was later marred by the revelation that the 'Lily' story had been a manufactured one, for which he served two months' imprisonment on a charge of technical abduction. But nothing could cloud his victory. Stead had forced through a major piece of legislation, fundamentally changing the law on morality.

The Criminal Law Amendment Act 1885: An Act to make further provision for the protection of women and girls, the suppression of brothels, and other purposes

Part 1: Protection of Women and Girls

2. Any person who:

(1) Procures or attempts to procure any girl or woman under twenty-one years of age, not being a common prostitute, or of known immoral character, to have unlawful carnal connexion, either within or without the Queen's dominions, with any other person or persons; or

(2) Procures or attempts to procure any woman or girl to become, either within or without the Queen's dominions, a common prostitute; or

(3) Procures or attempts to procure any woman or girl to leave the United Kingdom with intent that she may become an inmate of a brothel elsewhere; or

(4) Procures or attempts to procure any woman or girl to leave her usual place of abode in the United Kingdom . . . with intent that she may, for the purposes of prostitution, become an inmate of a brothel within or without the Queen's dominions,

shall be guilty of a misdemeanour, and being convicted thereof shall be liable at the discretion of the court to be imprisoned for any term not exceeding two years, with or without hard labour . . .

3. Any person who:

(1) By threats or intimidation procures or attempts to procure any woman or girl to have unlawful carnal connexion, either within or without the Queen's dominions; or

(2) By false pretences or false representations procures any woman or girl, not being a common prostitute or of known immoral character, to have any unlawful carnal connexion, either within or without the Queen's dominions; or

(3) Applies, adminsters to, or causes to be taken by any woman or girl any drug, matter, or thing, with intent to stupefy or overpower so as thereby to enable any person to have unlawful carnal connexion with such woman or girl,

shall be guilty of a misdemeanour, and being convicted thereof shall be liable at the discretion of the court to be imprisoned for any term not exceeding two years, with or without hard labour . . .

4. Any person who:

unlawfully and carnally knows any girl under the age of thirteen years shall be guilty of felony, and being convicted thereof shall be liable at the discretion of the court to be kept in penal servitude for life, or for any term not less than five years, or to be imprisoned for any term not exceeding two years, with or without hard labour . . .

5. Any person who:

(1) Unlawfully and carnally knows or attempts to have unlawful carnal knowledge of any girl being of or above the age of thirteen years and under the age of sixteen years; or

(2) Unlawfully and carnally knows, or attempts to have unlawful carnal knowledge of any female idiot or imbecile woman or girl, under circumstances which do not amount to rape, but which prove that the offender knew at the time of the commission of the offence that the woman or girl was an idiot or imbecile,

shall be guilty of a misdemeanour, and being convicted thereof shall be liable at the discretion of the court to be imprisoned for any term not exceeding two years, with or without hard labour . . .

6. Any person who, being the owner or occupier of any premises, or having, or acting or assisting in, the management or control thereof

induces or knowingly suffers any girl of such age as is in this section mentioned to resort to or be in or upon such premises for the purpose of being unlawfully and carnally known by any man, whether such carnal knowledge is intended to be with any particular man or generally,

(1) shall, if such girl is under the age of thirteen years, be guilty of felony, and

being convicted thereof shall be liable at the discretion of the court to be kept in penal servitude for life, or for any term not less than five years, or to be imprisoned for any term not exceeding two years, with or without hard labour; and

(2) if such girl is of or above the age of thirteen and under the age of sixteen years,

shall be guilty of a misdemeanour, and being convicted thereof shall be liable at the discretion of the court to be imprisoned for any term not exceeding two years, with or without hard labour . . .

7. Any person who:

with intent that any unmarried girl under the age of eighteen years should be unlawfully and carnally known by any man, whether such carnal knowledge is intended to be with any particular man, or generally takes or causes to be taken such girl out of the possession and against the will of her father or mother, of any other person having the lawful care or charge of her, shall be guilty of a misdemeanour, and being convicted thereof shall be liable at the discretion of the court to be imprisoned for any term not exceeding two years, with or without hard labour . . .

8. Any person who detains any woman or girl against her will:

(1) In or upon any premises with intent that she may be unlawfully and carnally known by any man, whether any particular man or generally, or

(2) In a brothel,

shall be guilty of a misdemeanour, and being convicted thereof shall be liable at the discretion of the court to be imprisoned for any term not exceeding two years, with or without hard labour . . .

12. Where on the trial of any offence under the Act it is proved to the satisfaction of the court that the seduction or prostitution of a girl under the age of sixteen has been caused, encouraged, favoured by her father, mother, guardian, master or mistress, it shall be in the power of the court to divest such father, mother, guardian, master or mistress of all authority over her, and to appoint any person or persons willing to take charge of such girl to be her guardian until she has attained the age of twenty-one, or any age below this as the court may direct, and the High Court shall have the power from time to time to rescind or vary such order by the appointment of any other person or persons as such guardian, or in any other respect.

Part II: Suppression of brothels

13. Any person who:

    (1) keeps or manages or acts or assists in the management of a brothel, or

    (2) being the tenant, lessee, or occupier of any premises, knowingly permits such premises or any part thereof to be used as a brothel or for the purposes of habitual prostitution, or

    (3) being the lessor or landlord of any premises, or the agent of such lessor or landlord, lets the same or any part thereof with the knowledge that such premises or some part thereof are or is to be used as a brothel. . . .

shall on summary conviction . . . be liable

    (1) to a penalty not exceeding twenty pounds, or, in the discretion of the court, to imprisonment for any term not exceeding three months, with or without hard labour, and,

    (2) on a second or subsequent conviction to a penalty not exceeding forty pounds, or in the discretion of the court, to imprisonment for any term not exceeding four months, with or without hard labour . . .

With the passing of the Criminal Law Amendment Act, the purity lobby had finally gained the ascendant. Any prospect of liberalising the law on prostitution was buried. Victorian values took on the final strain of puritanical and repressive puritanism for which they are known. The victory of moral purity would shape attitudes toward prostitution for the rest of Victoria's reign and beyond.

10. The Puritan Triumph

As the Criminal Law Amendment Bill became law, the moral purity lobby seized the opportunity to exploit their enormous good fortune. Moral purity activists had been lobbying fruitlessly throughout the nineteenth century for measures to attack vice in general, and prostitution in particular. The Act of 1885 gave them the breakthrough they had long desired and they moved rapidly to ensure they would secure hegemony over public morality.

A week after the Act became law, puritan leaders held a meeting in St James Hall, London, in order to form a new anti-vice organisation capable of enforcing the measures contained in the Act. Puritans entertained not unreasonable fears that the government would not enforce the Act unless pressure was applied. At the instigation of James Stansfeld the meeting resolved 'That this conference recommend the formation of a National Vigilance Association of men and women for the enforcement and improvement of the laws for the repression of criminal vice and public immorality'. This resolve was reinforced the next day, Saturday 22 August, by a huge demonstration in Hyde Park variously estimated as having attracted between 100,000 and a quarter of a million people.

Thus the most effective puritan organisation of the nineteenth century was created. The National Vigilance Association brought together the Society for the Suppression of Vice, the Minors' Protection Society, the Belgian Traffic Committee (Chair Benjamin Scott) and later the Central Vigilance Society. Many of the veterans of the anti-CD Law campaign went over to the new organisation. Josephine Butler joined, but was increasingly appalled by the repressive intolerance shown by the victorious puritans. Her libertarian objections were, however, swamped in the rising tide of puritan agitation.

In the first twelve months 105 prosecutions were undertaken, dealing with (a) disorderly houses (brothels), (b) men for offences against women, and (c) dealers in indecent books. The willingness of the NVA to take prosecutions had a marked effect on the moral activities of the state. In 1916 the long-serving secretary of the NVA, W.A. Coote, commented in *A Romance of Philanthropy* (p. 24) on the 'great change which now appertains to the authorities in this direction. To-day, they do their work so thoroughly and enthusiastically that very little legal work is left to the

Association.' This was in large part due to the work of the NVA in the years immediately after the passing of the Act, and in particular to their success in developing a national network of active Vigilance groups. The work of the NVA was crucial in creating a puritan hegemony over prostitution.

In setting up its national network, the advice given in the following article and the pamphlet mentioned in it were of crucial importance. *The Sentinel* was a hard-line puritan journal published by the Dyer Brothers (not to be confused with *The Shield*, the journal of the anti-CD Law campaign). This article was published in the February 1886 edition, p.18. [eio]

How to Form Local Vigilance Associations

In reply to applications for information as to what are the practical steps to be taken to form a local Vigilance Association, we beg to summarise briefly the steps which may be taken.

First: Formation of a Vigilance Association

Put yourself in communication, by writing a letter to your local newspaper or otherwise, with those who are willing to co-operate. Then write letters to all persons who are likely to assist, and to all moral, religious, and philanthropic bodies in your locality, asking the latter to send their representatives in order that all may meet together to discuss the advisability of forming such an Association. If it is decided upon, then hold a public meeting, and enlist as much popular support as possible.

Secondly: Organisation of a Vigilance Association

The organisation of the Association can hardly be too simple. Enrol as many men and women as possible as members, with a minimum subscription, and a pledge to co-operate in the furtherance of the objects of the Association. Appoint a working Executive Committee, with Chairman, Treasurer, and Honorary Secretary, and get to work.

Thirdly: the Work of a Vigilance Association

(A) Direct enforcement of the laws, local and general, for the repression of criminal vice and public immorality; (B) the removal of causes which contribute to the creation and maintenance of the evils complained of.

(A) The crimes which a Vigilance Committee will especially aim at suppressing are (1) the corruption and prostitution of girls under sixteen; (2) the abduction of girls under eighteen; (3) the procuration of the seduction of girls under twenty-one; (4) the fraudulent seduction of women of any age; (5) the entrapping or inveigling of girls or women into brothels; (6) the procuring of women for foreign brothels; and (7) the detention of women in houses of ill-fame.

The Vigilance Committee should also consider the question of enforcing the law for the suppression of brothels and of street solicitation. Ascertain what the law is. Look round and see where it is being broken. Distribute leaflets explaining what the law is. If that fails, set about securing evidence that can be produced in courts to punish lawbreakers. *Never begin a prosecution until you are certain that you have legal evidence and not mere rumour to justify your action.* The Central Association will be glad to give assistance and advice when consulted.

(B) In dealing with the causes which contribute to vice and immorality, first ascertain the facts. The co-operation of working women and the wives of working men, whose daughters have left or are leaving school, is essential. Ascertain the actual temptations and snares, then seek to reduce them. Among many lines of action the following may be suggested:

(1) Warning girls against employers of known immoral character; (2) The exposure of fraudulent and the establishment of honest register offices; (3) Providing respectable lodgings near, or making their existence known in, every railway station; (4) Opening places of refuge where girls locked out at night may find shelter; (5) The closing of immoral casinos and music halls; (6) Promoting opportunities, and where possible the establishment, of places for social intercourse and recreation; (7) Discouragement of customs and institutions such as hirings, &c, tending to immorality; (8) Inducing employers to provide lavatories and other conveniences for girls in their service; (9) Discouraging the sale and circulation of immoral literature, prints and pictures, and the insertion of immoral advertisements in the papers; and (10) urging teachers and others to be vigilant in checking laxity of morals among their scholars.

It is far from necessary that a Vigilance Committee should undertake all these lines of work. Some of them may be better undertaken by other agencies.

In dealing with all these questions it is well to remember that mere suppression of what is bad is of little use unless you put something that is good in its place.

The pamphlet 'Vigilance Committees and their Work' contains the text of the new law, together with some hints which may be useful as to the best method of enforcing its provisions. Further information on specific points may be obtained, with copies of this circular, on application to

Ralph Thicknesse, Hon. Secretary, W.A. Coote, Organising Secretary,

Office of the National Vigilance Association, 36, Strand, London.

While the NVA was building a most formidable organisation, the final repeal of the Contagious Diseases Acts took place on 26 March 1886. Ironically, the final victory owed less to the long campaign against the Acts than to parliamentary manoeuvre. Gladstone's third ministry was wracked by dissension over Irish Home Rule and Gladstone knew that Joseph Chamberlain was about to resign over the issue. The only obvious replacement was Sir James Stansfeld. But Stansfeld would not join the cabinet while the CD Acts remained on the statute book. Gladstone accordingly pushed through a repeal Act, and Stansfeld joined the cabinet just in time to see the Government collapse.

But while the Conservatives returned to power in the ensuing General Election, the reinstatement of the CD Acts was never contemplated. The 1885 Act remained on the statute books as an eloquent testimony to the way moral purity now dominated the debate on morality. Debate on prostitution steadily faded as Victorian values in their most oppressive form took shape. Socialists and other fringe groups attempted to keep debate alive, but as George Bernard Shaw and his socialist allies discovered, in late Victorian and Edwardian Britain this was an uphill task.

For a brief period, the 'Maiden Tribute' campaign had built a very wide base of support. It reached many working class and socialist organisations, attracting many trade unionists, and the great demonstration of 22 August was largely supported by working class Londoners protesting the sexual exploitation of their women folk by rich men. Stead had hoped to build on this a permanent alliance of the left and the centre. In the editorial introducing the 'Maiden Tribute', he had argued that 'The future belongs to the combined forces of Democracy and Socialism, which when united are irresistible. Divided on many points they will combine in protesting against the continued immolation of the daughters of the people as a sacrifice to the vices of the rich.' (*Pall Mall Gazette*, 6 July 1885, p. 1).

For a time this appeared likely. Two representatives of the Marxist Social Democratic Federation sat on the platform at the St James Hall meeting of 21 July. George Bernard Shaw had helped sell the *Pall Mall Gazette* on the streets during the 'Maiden Tribute' campaign. William Morris corresponded with Stead. But the socialists and trade unionists soon fell away. Shaw and his Fabian comrades were disgusted by the revelation that the 'Lily' story was a contrived one, and by Stead's

PRICE SIXPENCE.

THE

ELIZA ARMSTRONG CASE:

BEING A VERBATIM REPORT

OF THE

PROCEEDINGS AT BOW STREET.

WITH

M<small>R</small>. STEAD'S SUPPRESSED DEFENCE.

WITH ILLUSTRATIONS.

"PALL MALL GAZETTE" OFFICE, 2, NORTHUMBERLAND STREET, STRAND, LONDON, W.C.
1885.

The title page of Stead's *Pall Mall Gazette* portrays Rebecca Jarrett in court, charged with the abduction of Eliza Armstrong in 1885. (*History Today*)

contemptuous attitude to prostitutes in general and Rebecca Jarrett in particular. The anti-vice campaign looked on Stead's imprisonment as martyrdom of a hero. The left did not. The Marxists turned away to focus on the plight of the unemployed. The Fabians identified the causes of prostitution as poor pay and lack of opportunities for women under capitalism, rather than moral failings. The divisions between socialists and moralists became irreconcilable.

But while socialists divided from moralists, they did not abandon the campaign. In 1894 Shaw brought out a most eloquent statement of the socialist position in his play *Mrs Warren's Profession*. Shaw was dabbling in the then fashionable Ibsenite social realism, but found no takers for his deeply unrespectable drama. The leading Ibsenite producer of the time, J. T. Grein, refused to consider staging the play because it might lead strong men to insanity and suicide, while Mrs Theodore Wright, who Shaw had earmarked to play Mrs Warren, rushed out of the room when Shaw read it to her, declaiming that 'not even in her own room could she speak the part to herself . . .' (Holroyd, *Bernard Shaw*, vol. 1, Penguin, 1990, p. 296). The play had to wait till 1925 before receiving a public performance in Britain. But while the play was never performed in the Victorian period, it stands in its own right as testimony of what advanced socialist opinion was thinking about prostitution at the time it was written.

The play centres on the relationship between Mrs Warren and her daughter Vivie. At the start of the play Vivie knows nothing about her father and little about her mother. Since childhood she has been boarded in England while her mother attended to business in Brussels and Vienna. In this extract she discovers what her mother's business is. The extract given here is from Act II. Vivie is cross-examining her mother to discover her history, and Mrs Warren has resisted so far giving any clues. Punctuation as in original.

Mrs Warren: Oh, it's easy to talk, very easy, isn't it? Here! Would you like to know what my circumstances were?
Vivie: Yes: you had better tell me. Won't you sit down?
Mrs Warren: Oh, I'll sit down; don't you be afraid . . . Do you know what your grandmother was?
Vivie: No
Mrs Warren: No you don't. I do. She called herself a widow, and had a fried fish shop down by the Mint, and kept herself and four daughters out of it. Two of us were sisters . . . The other two were only half sisters; undersized, ugly, starved looking, hard working, honest poor creatures: Liz and I would have half murdered them if mother hadn't half-murdered us to keep our hands off them. They were the respectable ones. Well, what did they get by their respectability?

I'll tell you. One of them worked in a whitelead factory twelve hours a day for nine shillings a week until she died of lead poisoning. She only expected to get her hands a little paralysed; but she died. The other was always held up to us as a model because she married a Government labourer in the Deptford victualling yard, and kept his room and the three children neat and tidy on eighteen shillings a week – until he took to drink. That was worth being respectable for, wasn't it?

Vivie (now thoughtfully attentive): Did you and your sister think so?

Mrs Warren: Liz didn't, I can tell you; she had more spirit. We both went to a church school . . . and we stayed there until Liz went out one night and never came back . . . the clergyman was always warning me that Lizzie'd end by jumping off Waterloo Bridge. Poor fool; that was all he knew about it! But I was more afraid of the whitelead factory than I was of the river . . . That clergyman got me a situation as scullery maid in a temperance restaurant where they sent out for anything you liked. Then I was waitress: then I went to the bar at Waterloo station; fourteen hours a day serving drinks and washing glasses for four shillings a week and my board. That was considered great promotion for me. Well, one wretched night, when I was so tired I could hardly keep myself awake, who should come up for a half of scotch but Lizzie, in a long fur coat, elegant and comfortable, with a lot of sovereigns in her purse.

Vivie (grimly): My aunt Lizzie!

Mrs Warren: Yes; and a very good Aunt to have, too. She's living down at Winchester now, close to the Cathedral, one of the most respectable ladies there. Chaperones girls to the County Ball, if you please. No river for Liz, thank you! You remind me of Liz a little: she was a first rate business woman – saved money from the beginning – never let herself look too like what she was – never lost her head or threw away a chance. When she saw I'd grown up good looking she said to me across the bar, 'What are you doing there, you little fool? wearing out your health and your appearance for other people's profit!' Liz was saving money then to take a house for herself in Brussels; and she thought we two could save faster than one. So she lent me some money and gave me a start . . . Why shouldn't I have done it? The house in Brussels was real high class. A much better place for a woman to be in than the factory where Anne Jane got poisoned. None of our girls were ever treated as I was treated in the scullery of that temperance bar, or at the Waterloo bar, or at home. Would you have had me stay in them, and become a worn out drudge before I was forty?

Vivie (Intensely interested by this time): No; but why did you choose that business? Saving money and good management will succeed in any business.

Mrs Warren: Yes, saving money. But where can a woman get the money to save in any other business? Could you save out of four shillings a week and keep yourself dressed as well? Not you . . . all we had was our appearance and our turn for pleasing men. Do you think we were such fools as to let other people trade in our good looks by employing us as shopgirls, or barmaids, or waitresses, when we could trade them in ourselves and get all the profits instead of starvation wages? Not likely.

Vivie: You were certainly quite justified – from the business point of view.

Mrs Warren: Yes; or any other point of view. What is any respectable girl brought up to do but to catch some rich man's fancy and get the benefit of his money by marrying him? – as if a marriage ceremony could make any difference in the right or wrong of the thing! Oh, the hypocrisy of the world makes me sick! Liz and I had to work and save and calculate just like other people; elseways we should be as poor as any good-for-nothing drunken waster of a woman who thinks her luck will last for ever. (With great energy) I despise such people; they've no character; and if there's a thing I hate in a woman, it's want of character. . . .

Vivie: Still, you consider it worthwhile. It pays.

Mrs Warren: Of course it's worth while to a poor girl, if she can resist temptation and is good looking and well conducted and sensible. It's far better than any other employment open to her. I always thought that oughtn't to be. It can't be right, Vivie, that there shouldn't be better opportunities for women. I stick to that: it's wrong. But it's so, right or wrong: and a girl must make the best of it. But of course it's not worth while for a lady. If you took to it you'd be a fool; but I should have been a fool if I'd taken to anything else.

Vivie (more and more deeply moved): Mother: suppose we were both as poor as you were in the old days, are you quite sure that you wouldn't advise me to try the Waterloo bar, or marry a labourer, or even go into the factory?

Mrs Warren (indignantly): Of course not. What sort of mother do you take me for! How could you keep your self respect in such starvation and slavery? And what's a woman worth? What's life worth? without self respect! . . . Don't you be led astray by people who don't know the world, my girl. The only way for a woman to provide for herself decently is for her to be good to some man that can afford to be good to her. If she's in his own station in life, let her make him marry her; but if she's far beneath him she can't expect it: why should she? it wouldn't be for her own happiness. Ask any lady in London society that has daughters; and she'll tell you the same, except that I tell you straight and she'll tell you crooked. That's all the difference.

Vivie (fascinated, gazing at her): My dear mother: you are a wonderful woman: you are stronger than all England. And are you really and truly not one wee bit doubtful – or – or – ashamed?

Mrs Warren: Well, of course, dearie, it's only good manners to be ashamed of it: it's expected of a woman. Women have to pretend to feel a great deal that they don't feel. . . . But I can't stand saying one thing when everyone knows I mean another. What's the use in such hypocrisy? If people arrange the world that way for women, there's no good pretending it's arranged the other way. No. I never was ashamed really. I consider I had a right to be proud of how we managed everything so respectably, and never had a word against us, and how the girls were so well taken care of. Some of them did very well: one of them married an ambassador. But of course now I daren't talk about such things: whatever would they think of us! (She yawns) Oh Dear! I do believe I'm getting sleepy after all. (She stretches herself lazily, thoroughly relieved by her explosion, and placidly ready for her night's rest.)

By the time Shaw came to write *Mrs Warren's Profession*, the Vigilance Lobby was totally dominant and making great strides in its campaign to eliminate prostitution. The atmosphere of repression which followed the 1885 Act was created largely by the successes of the National Vigilance Association in local campaigns against brothels, and the changes in police attitudes which derived from these. The relative toleration of prostitution by the authorities in mid-century ceased. In the ten years before the Criminal Law Amendment Act legalised summary prosecutions of brothels, there was an annual average of 86 prosecutions of bawdy houses in England and Wales. Between 1885 and 1914 this average jumped to over 1,200 (Trevor Fisher, *Scandal*, Sutton Publishing, 1995, p. 162).

In Manchester a Vigilance Committee had been formed as early as 1882. The police had foolishly admitted to knowing of 402 brothels. The Vigilance Committee led a crusade against bawdy houses, and ten years later the police admitted to knowing of only three. This was certainly an underestimate but the trend was clear. Other towns followed suit, with a particularly vigorous campaign in the East End of London. There prostitutes were forced by the closing of brothels to pursue their trade on the streets and in the alley ways of Whitechapel and its surroundings, with grisly results. The Jack the Ripper murders in 1888 were directly attributable to Vigilance campaigns in the East End, which had driven the poorest and most degraded prostitutes to take their clients into dark and dangerous backyards.

The attitudes of the police towards street prostitutes were harsh, repressive and contemptuous. They realised that where street walkers were concerned, respectable society was wholly indifferent to what they did. A glimpse into police repression and its resultant perjury and corruption, is provided by two extraordinary cases in the autumn of 1895 when police overstepped the mark and arrested two articulate and respectable middle class men who were not willing to suffer in silence. Professor Ray

Lankester of Oxford University was arrested for obstruction in October after witnessing and protesting against the brutal arrest of a prostitute. The following month George Alexander, the leading theatrical manager of his era, was arrested and charged with an indecent act with a prostitute. Their testimony lifts the veil from police practices and court behaviour in the 1890s, revealing a significant transformation from the benign neglect of prostitution discussed by Howard Vincent in 1881 and the toleration exhibited by magistrates in the 1840s.

The Times, *7 October 1895*

At Marlborough Street, on Saturday, Edwin Ray Lankester, 48, described as a Professor of Anatomy . . . was charged with having been disorderly, and with resisting the police . . . Constable Wise deposed that shortly after 1 o'clock that morning he was on duty in Piccadilly near St James' Hall. He saw the defendant, in company with six or seven women of loose character, and therefore went up to them and requested them to pass along. The defendant turned to the women and said 'Don't you go; you remain here.' Witness again asked him to pass along, when the defendant said 'I shall not', and continued in conversation with the women. The witness then told him that he was obstructing him in the execution of his duty, and that if he did not go away he would have to take him into custody . . . The defendant turned round, and looking him in the face said 'I shall not go' . . . The witness then took him into custody . . .

Cross-examined by Sir George Lewis – Mr Lankester said at the police station that he thought he had a right to stop where he did and with anybody he liked . . . The defendant did say that a woman had been arrested and that he stopped to enquire what was the matter, but he did not hear him say that several of the women moved away and that he (the defendant) was left alone speaking to one woman . . . All the women moved off after the defendant was taken into custody. Witness thought Mr Lankester had been drinking and did not appear perfectly sober. He did not prefer a charge of drunkenness against him . . .

Constable Hutchins . . . said that he was with the first witness and saw the whole affair. He gave a corroborative account of the matter . . . In cross-examination the witness said he thought five minutes elapsed between the time the defendant was spoken to and his arrest. The women did not move away, and he thought six or eight of them were standing around when Mr Lankester was arrested . . .

Lankester wrote to *The Times* to protest against the impression left by the initial hearing, notably the allegation that he had not been sober and was carousing with the prostitutes. He argued, 'I need hardly say that an Oxford professor does not "laugh and talk" in the public thoroughfare with groups of prostitutes. My attempt to make inquiries of one such woman had a serious motive, and was due to my having witnessed the arrest . . . of another unhappy woman' (*The Times*, 7 October 1895).

Lankester was found guilty of obstruction and bound over on 12 October. The magistrate showed such partiality towards the police that Sir George Lewis retired from the case, arguing 'It seems to me, Sir, that you have absolutely made up your mind . . . instead of listening to any argument . . . you have interposed at every moment, and I will therefore retire from the case.' (*The Times*, 14 October 1895, p. 13). A furious Lankester had the last word on the subject with a long letter to *The Times* published in the same edition.

Lankester's letter to *The* Times, *14 October 1895*

. . . On my way from my club I stopped to ask some woman the explanation of an unusual scene of cruelty which I had witnessed. Before I had time to get an answer I was brusquely accosted by a policeman, and within three minutes (according to his own statement) seized by both arms and taken to a police station . . . I was put into a cell and kept two hours until I got bail . . . The sole point on which there is a conflict of evidence is as to what happened during the three minutes between my first being addressed by the policeman and the time of my arrest. He states that I obstructed him, but this I deny absolutely . . .

I ask whether it is tolerable that a man perfectly well known, talking to another person in the street (the character of the other person does not come into question, as there is no suggestion that any disturbance occurred), should be ordered to move on, and that on his remonstrating – even if angrily – he should be liable to be seized and treated as the vilest criminal?

It is time that a departmental enquiry was held, in view of the allegations of violence and concerted perjury which have been repeatedly made against a portion of the police. These are not the only charges made, for it is a matter of common report that they levy blackmail on the women of the street, and receive bribes from persons who they have arrested . . .

I confess that I am suffering keenly from a sense of the indignity inflicted on me and the attitude adopted by the magistrate – an attitude founded, as he himself was good enough to explain, on the fact that he had for twenty years sat on the Marlborough Street bench and had made it his custom to believe similar statements made to him by these same two constables. Mr Newton told me I was making a mountain out of a molehill . . . [he] cannot be ignorant that

. . . I was defending myself from the most odious and injurious statements as to drunkenness and association with disorderly characters . . .

Lankester's call for a departmental enquiry into police corruption fell on deaf ears. Most respectable people took the view of the Marlborough Street magistrate that police integrity was beyond question in a case involving prostitutes. Little over a month later, however, an even more remarkable case of police tactics was heard in the London courts, when George Alexander, proprietor of the St James Theatre, was charged with indecent behaviour.

'The Case of George Alexander', The Times,

5 November 1895

At Westminster yesterday, Mr George Alexander, theatrical manager, and Elizabeth Davis, 24, were charged with misconduct at Pavilion Rd, Chelsea. . . . Constable 284 B deposed that between 12 and 1 yesterday (Monday) morning he saw the prisoners in Pavilion Road . . . behaving in an improper way. Witness had indiarubber on his boots, and got within five yards of them before they noticed him. . . . Mr Dutton [counsel for the defence] said that he did not charge the policeman with making wilful mistatements . . . but he had made a grievous mistake . . . The defendant had just left his wife and had gone from his house – not twenty yards away – to call on a gentleman with whom he had important business. The unfortunate creature charged with him begged from him, implored him to help her, as she was starving. Mr Alexander put his hand in his pocket and gave her a coin, and for this he was locked up and disgraceful conduct imputed to him . . . Mr Alexander Wedderburn, barrister, deposed that it was to his house in Cadogan Place that Mr Alexander was going to make a call. He had known the defendant for twenty years as a man of irreproachable character . . . Mr A.W. Pinero, the dramatic author, and others gave evidence as to character, Mr Pinero's estimate being that Mr Alexander was a 'very high minded man' . . . Mr de Rutzen [the magistrate] said he would have liked evidence as to when the defendant left his own house. What interval of time elapsed before his arrest? This was not before him. The police had given their evidence in a most satisfactory way, but he would give the defendant Alexander the benefit of the doubt and discharge him. The woman, who had admitted the offence, and who . . . was a nightly loiterer in the locality, would enter into her recognizances for future good behaviour.

Although Alexander had been acquitted, the circumstances led him to write to *The Times*. In the course of his letter, he stated that the constable had alleged he had had connection with the woman – a remarkable statement which, if repeated in court, would have raised the stakes considerably.

'The Charge against Mr George Alexander', The Times, 5 November 1895

Sir – As the law prevented my giving evidence on oath on my own behalf at the police court yesterday, I hope you will allow me to make a statement . . . On the night of the 3rd November I went out with the intention of posting a letter to a friend – Mr Wedderburn – when it occurred to me to go to his house in Cadogan place . . . On approaching his house I saw no light, so I turned back towards home, and when I got to Hans Street a woman accosted me, caught me by the arm, and solicited me. I could, even in the dim light, see that the woman was poor, miserable, starved and ill clad, so I put my hand in my pocket and gave her the first coin that I came across . . . She was walking by my side when a constable came up between me and her and said 'Why are you loitering here?' . . . He then said, 'I saw you having connexion with this woman in the Pavilion Road', and the woman said, 'I am not going to deny it.' I said to the constable, 'Do you know realise what you are saying? My name is George Alexander. I live at 37 Pont Street, and my wife is there now. Let us go there.' He said, 'No, you will have to go to the station . . . I then walked peacefully by his side, telling him that he had no need to grip my arm in any way. On arriving at the station I gave my name and address to the inspector, who then charged me . . .

Two days after his acquittal Alexander appeared on the stage of his St James's Theatre and was cheered by the audience. By a happy chance, the play was *Liberty Hall*. Alas, the freedom to walk the streets had been severely circumscribed by the anti-prostitute crusade. Paradoxically, a similar form of harassment of street woman which had been associated with the legalisation of prostitution under the Contagious Diseases Acts was now being carried out in the name of the repression of prostitution. But by the 1890s, there was no Josephine Butler to contest the abuse of power by the police.

The final piece of legislation against prostitution in the Victorian era was the 1898 Vagrancy Act. Despite its title, it was in fact aimed against pimps, as a moral panic had emerged in the late 1890s over men living off immoral earnings.

An Act to amend the Vagrancy Act 1824 (12 August 1898)

Be it enacted . . . as follows:

1. (1) Every male person who:
   (a) knowingly lives wholly or in part on the earnings of prostitution; or
   (b) in any public place persistently solicits or importunes for immoral purposes,

shall be deemed a rogue and vagabond within the meaning of the Vagrancy Act, 1824, and may be dealt with accordingly.

(2) If it is made to appear to a court of summary jurisdiction by information on oath that there is reason to suspect that any house or any part of a house is used by a female for purposes of prostitution, and that any male person residing in or frequenting the house is living wholly or in part on the earnings of the prostitute, the court may issue a warrant authorising any constable to enter and search the house and to arrest that male person.

(3) Where a male person is proved to live with or to be habitually in the company of a prostitute and has no visible means of subsistence, he shall, unless he can satisfy the court to the contrary, be deemed to be knowingly living on the earnings of prostitution . . .

The repressive policies which emerged after the 1885 Criminal Law Amendment Act did not, of course, remove prostitution. Women continued to follow the oldest profession, many driven by the economic pressures described by Shaw in *Mrs Warren's Profession*. Men, many of them highly respectable middle class males, continued to use prostitutes. Professor Lankaster and George Alexander may have been wrongly accused, but working class policemen had no reason to think that a respectable middle class male could not be a client of a prostitute. And inevitably, the result was the continuation of venereal disease as a major problem. VD was the spectre at the feast of Victorian society.

When the suffragettes broke through the taboos surrounding women's position in contemporary society, the taboo against discussing the issue was one they confronted. Christabel Pankhurst broke the taboo with her pamphlet *The Great Scourge and how to end it* in 1913, based on articles in *The Suffragette*. Her polemic was strident and her linkage of 'Votes for women and chastity for men' was simplistic, but she undoubtedly focused on an issue of major importance in the history of sexuality. That the debate on venereal disease was not simply of interest to suffragettes was shown in the same year when the government set up a Royal

Commission on the subject. Prostitution and venereal disease were two sides of the same coin. Throughout the 'long' nineteenth century from the 1790s to the outbreak of the First World War, the coin had been repeatedly spun and spun again. It is spinning still.

'The Great Scourge and how to end it', Christabel Pankhurst LL.B.

pp. v–xi

This book deals with what is commonly described as the Hidden Scourge, and is written with the intention that this scourge shall be hidden no longer, for if it were to remain hidden, then there would be no hope of abolishing it.

Men writers for the most part refuse to tell what the Hidden Scourge is, and so it becomes the duty of women to do it. The Hidden Scourge is sexual disease, which takes two chief forms – syphilis and gonorrhoea. These diseases are due to prostitution – they are due, that is to say, to sexual immorality. But they are not confined to those who are immoral. Being contagious, they are communicated to the innocent, and especially to wives. The infection of innocent wives in marriage is justly declared by a man doctor to be the 'the crowning infamy of our social life'.

Generally speaking, wives who are thus infected are quite ignorant of what is the matter with them. The men who would think it indelicate to utter in their hearing the words syphilis and gonorrhoea, seem not to think it indelicate to infect them with the terrible diseases which bear these names . . .

To discuss an evil, and then to run away from it without suggesting how it may be cured, is not the way of Suffragettes, and in the following pages will be found a proposed cure for the great evil in question. That cure, briefly stated, is Votes for Women and Chastity for Men. Quotations and opinions from eminent men are given, and these show that chastity for men is healthful for themselves and is imperative in the interests of the race . . .

The opponents of votes for women know that women, when they are politically free and economically strong, will not be purchasable for the base uses of vice. Those who want to have women as slaves obviously do not want women to become voters. All the high sounding arguments against giving votes for women are a sham – a mere attempt to cover up the real argument against this reform, which argument, we repeat, is sexual vice . . .

'Plain Facts about a Great Evil', pp. 38–48
As might be expected, the statements that we make as to sexual disease and its

causes evoke a good deal of comment on the part of men. Some men say they completely endorse our statements of fact . . . Other men offer criticism. These critics say . . . that our statements as to the prevalence of sexual disease amongst men are exaggerated. In the second place, they say that the reason of [sic] men's vice is an economic one, and that if men could afford to marry they would no longer have intercourse with prostitutes. It is, of course, principally Socialist men who adopt this second line of argument.

There is a complete answer to both these objections. Firstly, as to the denial of our assertion that 75 per cent to 80 per cent of men contract gonorrhoea . . . The assertion in question is not made upon our own authority, but upon that of medical men . . . Noeggerath says that in New York, out of 1,000 married men, 800 have had gonorrhoea, and that 90 per cent of these have not been healed and can infect their wives. Ricord also says the 80 per cent of men contract gonorrhoea, and says further: 'When anyone has once acquired gonorrhoea, God only knows when he will get well again . . . Dr A. Prince Morrow, author of *Social Diseases and Marriage*, says: 'Gonorrhoea is the most widespread and universal of all diseases in the adult male population, embracing 75 per cent or more . . .'

Dr Douglas White, MD, and Dr C.H. Melville, of the Royal Army Medical Corps, who jointly prepared a paper on venereal disease read at the Annual Congress of the Royal Institute of Public Health, said 'The majority of all young men get gonorrhoea before the age of thirty'. These statements of fact may be supplemented by two further statements. One is that, as James Foster Scott MD, expresses it, 'In every case where a woman is infected with gonorrhoea, she is in danger not only of being rendered a permanent invalid and barren, but also of losing her life from peritonitis and septicaemia.' In mild cases a woman suffers from that 'poor health' that is falsely supposed to be Nature's gift to women. In severe cases the sex organs have to be removed by the surgeon's knife. Dr Prince Morrow says: 'All modern writers on the diseases of women recognise that *gonorrhoea is the chief determining cause of the inflammatory diseases peculiar to women.*' . . .

To reply to the statement of our critics who say that the reason of [sic] sexual vice is an economic one, and that if all men could afford to marry, prostitution would disappear. That this contention is unfounded is proved by these facts. Firstly, that rich men, who can perfectly well afford to marry, are quite as immoral as poor men. Secondly, that married men as well as unmarried men have intercourse with prostitutes. The problem of vice is certainly an economic one in this sense, that where women are economically dependent upon men, they more readily become the victims of vice . . . If a woman can earn an adequate living by the work of her hand or brain, then it will be much the harder to compel her to earn her living by selling her sex.

Here we have the reason why a man-made Socialism is not less dangerous to women than man-made Capitalism. So long as men have the monopoly of political power, it will be impossible to restrain their impulse to keep women in economic dependence and so sexually subservient. In this sense, as we have said, the question of White Slavery is an economic one . . .

And there is another infamous thing to be told. The men, married and unmarried, who visit bad houses are not content to degrade women of full age and mature physical development. They want young girls, and, if they can get them, virgins. Bernard Shaw, in his preface to 'Three Plays by Brieux', cites Brieux's contention . . . that no man likes to face the responsibility of tempting a girl to her first step from the beaten path. Mr Shaw is behind the times, for at the present day it is, as the White Slaves can tell us, 'a perfect craze with men' to have intercourse with the youngest possible girl, and they are especially eager to be the first to ruin her . . .

The fact is that it is no longer any use for men to try to preserve the illusions of the virtuous woman as to what goes on in the underworld. This men must now accept. A double standard of morality means that they will be more and more cast out by self-respecting women. Until men accept the same moral standard as women, how can it be said that they are fit companions for them?

The virtuous woman has often been condemned for shrinking from her 'fallen' sister and holding out the hand of friendship to the fallen man. Not much longer will women continue to deserve that reproach, because they have come to the conclusion that men are not worthy to associate with them who are not of clean mind and clean life.

Epilogue: Debating the Unmentionable

Historical interpretations of Victorian morality are in a welcome state of uncertainty. The old polarities between a vision of the Victorians as embracing a hegemonic puritan code, or paying lipservice to the code while breaking it systematically, will not do. In no area is this more so than in prostitution, an area still often seen as being unmentionable in the Victorian period. As this book has shown, for most Victorians a discreet silence may have been *de rigueur*, but for opinion-makers among politically active sections of society the unmentionable was scrutinised with rigour and intensity throughout the nineteenth century.

The historical record shows that a complex pattern of attitudes towards prostitution existed in the 'long' nineteenth century. A relaxed, even cynical toleration of the phenomenon survived from the eighteenth century, despite the growing influence of a puritanically inclined militancy among evangelical Christians. This militancy was a constant presence from the 1830s onward, leading to the almost obsessive dissection of the phenomenon detailed in the early part of this book, and the sustained attempts to change the law shown by puritans in the first half of the nineteenth century. Yet, as the evidence shows, the puritans were unable to convince legislators that tightening the law was desirable, and *laissez faire* remained dominant.

The paradox of the mid-Victorian period is that while Respectability made substantial inroads into most areas of life, it made no impact at all where prostitution was concerned. Indeed, as the evidence given above clearly shows, the puritan failure to move legislators in their direction in the 1840s opened the way for the public health lobby to secure moves toward the legalisation of prostitution. The advances made in this regard via the Contagious Diseases Acts speaks volumes about the weakness of the anti-vice campaign when faced with the quiet but intransigent opposition of the male elite. The political failings of the moral purity campaign are illustrated by the legislative campaigns of 1844 and 1849, and go part of the way to explaining why this was so. The massive extent of vice among upper class males demonstrated by the debate on the *demi-monde* in the 1860s provides another piece of the jigsaw. Yet there remains much to be explained.

The puritans themselves pointed to the contrast between their success in restricting gambling and their failure in the realm of prostitution. Like temperance reform,

The London Female Guardian Society seeks to rescue fallen women and restore them to Jesus. (Advertisement in *Punch*, 1926. Mary Evans Picture Library)

prostitution remained an area where puritanism could not make any headway. This was in part because the Conservative Party remained totally indifferent to puritan concerns, but a more important factor was the almost equal indifference of Gladstonian Liberalism. Moral puritans, who were overwhelmingly Liberal in political sympathies, felt this failure as an almost personal betrayal. In the 1870s they came to hate the Liberals far more deeply than the Conservatives, with disastrous results. Even in the early 1880s, when Stansfeld targeted the Liberal Party with success, most Liberal MPs were lukewarm or hostile. It was only through marshalling limited strength with great political skill that Stansfeld secured the defeat of the CD Laws.

Why the Liberals were so deeply resistant is an issue which has yet to be explored. Part of the reason must lie in the attitudes to prostitution of leading Liberal politicians, which were liberal in all senses. Hartington, sometime leader of the Liberal party in the 1870s, carried memories of his relationship with Skittles to deter him from puritanism. Gladstone himself pursued prostitutes in the streets of London, ostensibly to reclaim them from a life of vice. The tolerance shown to the Liberal leader in this curious practice at a time when he was chancellor of the exchequer, and on his way to becoming prime minster, is not the least puzzling aspect of the mid-Victorian tolerance of prostitution.

Gladstone. (Carlo Pellegrini;
by courtesy of the National
Portrait Gallery, London)

Yet the puritans broke through spectacularly in the 1880s. Like the battle of Waterloo, the victory of 1885 was a close-run affair. Benjamin Scott snatched victory from the jaws of defeat only by enlisting the help of a newspaper editor whose cavalier regard for the facts and willingness to turn a political campaign into a moral crusade has damned him in the eyes of posterity. Yet Stead was not the political fanatic he has often been portrayed as being. He assessed the political situation with a shrewd eye to possibilities, mobilised the support offered by Josephine Butler and the leaders of the Salvation Army, and, most crucially, was prepared to challenge the hypocrisy of the late Victorian political elite.

The moral puritans had won the case over white slavery as early as the report of the Lords select committee in 1882. That three Bills failed to pass the Commons had much to do with the hypocrisy of a political class which, while regularly deploring the existence of prostitution, was not prepared to do anything about it. Moral puritans had long believed that there was corruption in high places, and that it was to defend this corruption that the political establishment was reluctant to take effective action against the brothel interest. The key fact about the Maiden Tribute Campaign is not that Stead manufactured the 'Lily' story, for which he was indeed later condemned and imprisoned, but that he challenged the government to prosecute him for obscenity, threatening to expose vice at the highest levels of British society. Faced with this threat the government immediately capitulated. Both front benches marched rapidly to pass the Criminal Law Amendment Bill with a rapidity suggesting acute political embarrassment.

The toleration of prostitution was thus insecurely founded. There is clearly some foundation for the accusations of hypocrisy made against the Victorians by critics such as Shaw and Strachey. Yet a simple charge of hypocrisy will not do. The very triumph of puritanism after 1885, in particular the success of the National Vigilance Association in changing police attitudes, demonstrates the strength of puritanism in Victorian Britain. The testimonies of Professor Lankester and George Alexander show the change in police attitudes from those reported by Howard Vincent a decade and a half earlier. The passing of the Vagrancy Law of 1898, with astonishingly little debate, makes the same point. Changes in attitude of so fundamental a nature do not happen unless there is an underlying groundswell of opinion which, once mobilised, sweeps all before it.

Gladstone himself was affected. Until the mid-1880s he could walk the streets accosting prostitutes with impunity. After the passing of the 1885 Act he could no longer do so. In 1886 his private secretary Sir Edward Hamilton and his foreign secretary Lord Rosebery warned him that the climate had changed and he must desist. The Grand Old Man reluctantly complied, commenting that 'there was among some people a baseness and lack of charity which enabled them to believe the worst. Because of this I will cease to visit clearing houses, brothels or places of assignation . . . and . . . promise never again to speak to women in the streets at night.'

From this point onwards, repressive attitudes towards prostitution became set in stone. Victorian Values at their most puritanical became the norm both legally and socially. And yet prostitution did not vanish, but merely disappeared into a semi-visible hinterland whose contours have yet to be explored. The dominance of Victorian Values in this form continued well into the twentieth century, but the debate on national degeneration which began in the *fin de siècle* atmosphere of the 1890s, and was reinforced by the venereal ravages during two world wars, was to erode the confident assumption of the moral purity lobby that prostitution could be eradicated.

The First World War ended their confidence in this area, as in so many others. Indeed, at the end of the twentieth century it is surprising how many of the debates covered in this book are still with us. Legalisation of prostitution or its continuing outlawing is a live issue. Kerb crawling and the protests of the inhabitants of red light districts against the nuisances which follow are regularly headline news. And most ominously, white slavery, juvenile prostitution and paedophilia seem if anything to be more serious problems at the end of the twentieth century than they were a century ago. The debates on prostitution conducted in the 'long' nineteenth century still resonate today.

The assessment of prostitution in the 'long' century throws a salutary light on the morality of Britain in the period. The evidence presented in this book clearly indicates that prostitution was a serious issue for serious Victorians. The popular images of a polite and respectable people, or a hypocritical and repressive society which did not practise what it preached, cannot be substantiated. Informed Victorians were perfectly well aware of the existence of the Great Social Evil, and discussed it at length. What they should do about it was deeply controversial and the eventual triumph of the puritans was by no means inevitable. The Victorian era was far more complex than a simple advance towards respectability and prudery. If Mrs Grundy and her hard-nosed associates eventually triumphed, this was only as part of a complex interplay of forces. This book has thrown some light on the interplay as the Victorians understood it through their own contemporary experiences and analyses, but there is much that remains obscure. The myth that the Victorians saw prostitution as an unmentionable subject must now, however, be consigned to oblivion.

Select Bibliography

Place of publication London, England, unless otherwise indicated.

Acton, William, *Prostitution: Considered in its Moral, Social and Sanitary Aspects, in London and other Large Cities: with Proposals for the Mitigation and Prevention of its Attendant Evils*, 1856, edited Peter Fryer, 1968 (Fitzroy edn), MacGibbon & Kee; 1870 edition, reprinted Frank Cass, 1972

Blyth, Henry, *Skittles, the Last Victorian Courtesan*, Rupert Hart-Davis, 1970

Bristow, Edward J., *Vice and Vigilance*, Gill & Macmillan, Dublin, 1977

Butler, Josephine Elizabeth, *Personal Reminiscences of a Great Crusade*, Horace Marshall, 1896

Collier, J., *The General Next to God, the Story of William Booth and the Salvation Army*, Collins, 1965

Cominos, Peter T., 'Late Victorian Sexual Respectability and the Social System', *International Review of Social History*, No. 8, 1963

Coote, W.A., *A Romance of Philanthropy*, National Vigilance Association, 1916

Davenport-Hines, Richard, *Sex, Death and Punishment*, Collins, 1990

Doig, Alan, *Westminster Babylon*, Allison & Busby, 1990

Dyer, Alfred, *The European Slave Trade in English Girls, A Narrative of Facts*, Dyer Brothers, Amen Corner, Paternoster Row, 1880

Ensor, R.C.K., *England 1870–1914*, Oxford History of England, Oxford, Clarendon Press, 1936/1990

Ereira, Alan, *The People's England*, Routledge & Kegan Paul, 1981

Finnegan, Frances, *Poverty and Prostitution, a Study of Victorian Prostitution in York*, Cambridge University Press, 1979

Fryer, Peter, *Mrs Grundy: Studies in English Prudery*, Denis Dobson, 1963

Gordham, Deborah, 'The "Maiden Tribute of Modern Babylon",' in *Victorian Studies* 21 (1978)

Harrison, Brian, 'Josephine Butler', in J.F.C. Harrison, B. Taylor and I. Armstrong (eds), *Eminently Victorian*, 1974

——, 'State Intervention and Moral Reform in Nineteenth Century England', in P. Hollis (ed.), *Pressure from Without in Early Victorian England*, Edward Arnold, 1974

Hemyng, Bracebridge, 'Prostitution in London', in Henry Mayhew (ed.), *London Labour and the London Poor*, Vol IV, Stationer's Hall Court, London, December 1861, Reprinted Frank Cass, 1967

Hudson, Derek, *Munby, Man of Two Worlds*, John Murray, 1972

Hyam, Ronald, *Empire and Sexuality*, Manchester University Press, 1990

Jenkins, Roy, *Gladstone*, MacMillan, 1995

Logan, William, *The Great Social Evil*, Hodder & Stoughton, 1871

McGlashan, W.J., *England on her Defence, a Reply to 'The Maiden Tribute of Modern Babylon'*, 1885

McHugh, Paul, *Prostitution and Victorian Social Reform*, Croom Helm, 1980

Marcus, Steven, *The Other Victorians*, Corgi/Bantam, 1969

Matthews, H.C.G., *Gladstone*, vol. 1 1809–1874, Oxford University Press, 1986

——, Gladstone, vol. 2 1875–1898, Oxford, Clarendon Press, 1995

Mazo Karras, Ruth, *Common Women: Prostitution and Sexuality in Medieval England*, Oxford University Press, 1996

Midgley, Clare, *Women against Slavery*, Routledge, 1992

Millett, Kate, *Sexual Politics*, Virago, 1977

Mort, Frank, *Dangerous Sexualities*, Routledge & Kegan Paul, 1987

Neild, Kenneth, *Prostitution in the Victorian Age*, ed. K. Neild, Gregg International Publishers, 1973; Reprints of key contemporary articles

Pearsall, Ronald, *The Worm in the Bud*, Weidenfeld & Nicolson, 1969

Pearson, Michael, *The Age of Consent*, David & Charles, 1972

Petrie, Glen, *A Singular Iniquity, the Campaigns of Josephine Butler*, Macmillan, 1971

Playfair, Giles, *Six Studies in Hypocrisy*, Secker & Warburg, 1969

Read, Donald, *England 1868–1914*, Longman, 1979

Report from the Royal Commission on the Contagious Diseases Acts 1871, British Parliamentary Papers, Irish University Press, Shannon, Ireland, Health, Infectious Diseases, Vol. 5

Scott, Benjamin, *A State Iniquity; Its Rise, Extension and Overthrow*, 1890/94, Kegan Paul, Trench, Trubner and Co., reprinted 1968, Augustus M. Kelley, New York

Seaman, L.C.B., *Victorian England*, Routledge, 1973

Showalter, Elaine, *Sexual Anarchy: Gender and Culture at the Fin de Siècle*, Indiana, Bloomsbury, 1991

Smith, F. Barry, 'Sexuality in Britain 1800–1900', in Martha Vincinus (ed.), *A Widening Sphere*, Bloomington and London, Indiana University Press, 1977

Stead, W.T., *The Armstrong Case: Mr Stead's Defence in Full*, printed and published W.T. Stead, 1885

——, *Speech of W.T. Stead at the Central Criminal Court, November 4th 1885*, Moral Reform Union, 1885

Terrot, Charles, *The Maiden Tribute*, Frederick Muller, 1979

Thane, Pat, *Late Victorian Women in Later Victorian Britain 1867–1900*, ed. T.R. Gourvish and Alan O'Day, Macmillan, 1990

Thompson, Dorothy, *Queen Victoria: Gender and Power*, Virago, 1990

Thompson, F.M.L., *The Rise of Respectable Society*, Fontana, 1988

Tingsten, Herbert, *Victoria and the Victorians*, George Allen & Unwin, 1972

Trudgill, Eric, *Madonnas and Magdalens*, Heinemann, 1976

Walkowitz, Judith R., *City of Dreadful Delight*, Virago, 1992

——, 'The Making of an Outcast Group', in Martha Vincinus, (ed.), *A Widening Sphere*, Bloomington and London, Indiana University Press, 1977

——, *Prostitution and Victorian Society*, Cambridge University Press, 1980

'Walter', *My Secret Life*, ed. Gordon Grinley, Panther, 1972

Weeks, Jeffrey, *Sex, Politics and Society*, Longman, 1981 and 1991 editions

Weintraub, Sidney, *Disraeli*, Hamish Hamilton, 1993

Weintraub, Stanley, *Victoria*, Unwin Hyman, 1987

Whyte, Frederick, *Life of W.T. Stead*, vol. 1, Jonathan Cape, 1925

Wilson, Angus, *The Naughty Nineties*, Eyre Methuen, 1976

Wood, Anthony, *Nineteenth Century Britain*, Longman, 1982

Woodward, L., *The Age of Reform*, 2nd edn, Oxford University Press, 1962

Index